THE GREAT DYING
THE BLACK DEATH IN DUBLIN

THE GREAT DYING
THE BLACK DEATH IN DUBLIN

MARIA KELLY

TEMPUS

First published 2003

Tempus Publishing Limited
The Mill, Brimscombe Port,
Stroud, Gloucestershire, GL5 2QG
www.tempus-publishing.com

British Library Cataloguing in Publication Data.
A catalogue record for this book is available from the British Library.

ISBN 0 7524 2338 X

Typesetting and origination by Tempus Publishing Limited
Printed in Great Britain by Midway Colour Print, Wiltshire

Contents

Acknowledgements

I would like to acknowledge with deep gratitude Mr Kenneth W. Nicholls, History Department, University College Cork, for his generosity in supplying me with a copy of Speed's Map of Dublin and permission to reproduce the same.

I would also like to acknowledge the Special Collections of the Boole Library, University College Cork, for the map from *Civitates Orbis Terrarum*.

I am deeply indebted to Helen Davis, Special Collections Librarian at University College Cork for her expertise and efficiency in locating the maps used in this book; to Dr Lawrence Stepelevich for his imaginative sketches; to Dermot Kelly for permission to reproduce his photographs; to Tempus staff, Jonathan Reeve for his unstinting enthusiasm and encouragement and Joanna de Vries for her efficient and friendly editorial help.

And, in alphabetical order – that other great leveller – my sincere thanks for their assistance in sundry ways go to the following: Dr Neil Buttimer (UCC), Lieve Dhaene, Patricia Kelly, Dr Sean Duffy (TCD), Dr Padraigín Riggs (UCC), and, as always, my family: William, Will, Hugh and Oisín.

Where are our dear friends now? Where are the beloved faces? Where are the affectionate words, the relaxed and enjoyable conversations? What lightning bolt devoured them? What earthquake toppled them? What tempest drowned them? What abyss swallowed them? There was a crowd of us, now we are almost alone. We should make new friends – but how, when the human race is almost wiped out; and why, when it looks to me as if the end of the world is at hand? Why pretend? We are alone indeed... How transient and arrogant an animal is man! How shallow the foundations on which he rears his towers! You see how our great band of friends has dwindled. Look, even as we speak we too are slipping away, vanishing like shadows. One minute someone hears that another has gone, the next he is following in his footsteps.

Go mortals, sweat, pant, toil, range the lands and seas to pile up riches you cannot keep; glory that will not last. The life we lead is a sleep; whatever we do, dreams. Only death breaks the sleep and wakes us from dreaming. I wish I could have woken before this.

Petrarch, Letters on Familiar Matters
to Louis Heyligen, Parma, May-June 1349.

CHAPTER ONE

In Search of the Black Death

THE EVIDENCE FOR THE BLACK DEATH
IN IRELAND

Between the fourteenth and the eighteenth centuries some 50 million Europeans are believed to have died of plague. Little wonder then that it has entered the mythology of European cities where the plague claimed most of its victims. European cities would experience other epidemics, but none was as devastating as the Black Death, which struck first in 1348 and then repeatedly throughout the rest of the century and for the following 200 years.

How cities throughout Europe responded to this threat has been richly documented. The great urban chroniclers, such as

Gilbert li Muisis in Tournai, Agnolo di Tura in Siena, Matteo Villani and Boccaccio in Florence and Petrarch in Parma, all offer moving details of the reactions of urban dwellers to this new and inescapable threat. For Dublin, we do not have any such chronicles, and only the Franciscan chronicler, Friar John Clyn, has left an eyewitness account of how people reacted to the plague of 1348. The other written sources are, for varying reasons, silent on the subject. The entries in the *Account Roll* of the Priory of Holy Trinity at Christ Church Cathedral in Dublin end just before the Black Death broke out in the city. Documents from the other great religious houses, such as the Hospital of St John the Baptist and the Abbey of St Thomas, are equally deficient in detail about the plague. The surviving manuscripts of the various annals collected in the *Chartularies of St Mary's Abbey, Dublin* offer little information. In one manuscript (TCD – MS E.3.11), which covers the period 1070-1427, there is a gap between 1222 and 1307 and again between 1316 and 1361; in the excerpts made by Sir James Ware in the seventeenth century, there is a break between 1337 and 1361; in the Laud MS, though the period from 1162 to 1370 is covered, the information provided about the Black Death and later outbreaks is cursory. Another chronicle to which Ware refers and which he attributed to Pembrig, a Dublin writer, finishes in 1347 with a terse '*Hic finitur Chronica Pembrig*'. The *Calendar of the Ancient Records of Dublin* does not offer any direct evidence of the plague of 1348. Nor is much information about Dublin available in the Irish annals, which were concerned primarily with Gaelic-Irish politics and politicians. To the native annalists, Dublin and other cities were, in the words of one historian, '...places where men die or are hanged, or imprisoned, places that are on occasion raided, hardly more'. There is relatively little documentation for late fourteenth-century Irish urban history, and those urban documents that do exist are concerned principally with the granting of privileges or with the lives of the rich and powerful.[1]

Archaeological evidence is almost as scant. Plague, along with other diseases such as smallpox or cholera, does not produce any pathognomonic or other changes in the bone and so osteoar-chaeological traces cannot be detected in skeletons. Therefore, though we know that medieval Irish people suf-fered from dental decay and arthritis, archaeology has not been able to discern if they died of plague and especially so if death occurred quickly. However, new techniques, espe-cially DNA-detection techniques, promise to yield more information. Mass plague graves, unearthed in other European cities, have not been found in Dublin, though an urban legend of unknown origin persists that the area of Blackpitts was once the site of mass graves or pits for Black Death victims. Thanks in part to extensive building in Georgian times and other factors, medieval Dublin itself has almost disappeared, leaving little trace except for its two cathedrals (which are now largely nineteenth-century renovations), a few churches, some street names and small sections of the town wall. Despite extensive archaeological work in the city, only a relatively small part of the medieval city has been excavated thus far and excavation findings, while affording insight into details of daily life, have yet to reveal anything directly relevant to the plague. In fact, there is a complete absence of stratified deposits from the later fourteenth and fifteenth centuries and ev-idence from pottery studies dwindles in the same period.

Tracing the history of the Black Death in Dublin, then, would seem an impossible task. Some might argue that the

A.D. 1346. Comes Kildarie, insurgunt mense Novembri contra
November. Omorda et suos complices qui castra prescripta de
Ley et Ky[l]mehede conbusserunt, et eum et suos
complices sic strenue cum suis exercitibus, prose-
quuntur, aggrediuntur et invadunt spoliando, necando,
et conburendo quod dictus Omorda et sui complices,
licet idem in principio cum multis millibus Hiberni-
corum fortiter eisdem et pertinaciter restitissent, in fine
compulsi se Regis gratie subjecerunt, et dicti Comitis
voluntati se totaliter reddiderunt.

*Castles of
Ley and
Kylme-
hede.*

A.D. 1347.   Anno Domini MCCCXLVII. — Comes Kildarie cum
Baronibus et militibus transfert se, mense Maii, ad
Regem Anglie, in sui adjutorium tunc apud Caleys
in obsidione existentem.

Calais.

Item, villa de Caleys per inhabitantes eodem quarto
die mensis Junii Regi Anglie redditur.

4 June.

Item, Walterus Bonevile, Willelmus Calfe, et Willelmus Welesley, et multi alii nobiles et validi, tam
de Anglia quam de Hibernia et Wallia, in infirmitate
constituti apud Caleys obierunt.

Item, Macmurgh, videlicet, Donaldus Macmurgh,
filius Donaldi Arte Macmurgh, Rex Lagenie, quinto
die mensis Junii per suos proditiose interficitur.

*King of
Leinster.*

5 June.

Item, Mauricius Filius Thome, Comes Kildarie, a
Rege Anglie miles instituitur.

*Earl of
Kildare.*

Item, dictus Comes filiam Domini Bartholomei de
Burwasse [Burghersh] in uxorem duxit.

Item, villa de Nanagh, que vocatur Nenagh, cum fol.
tota patria adjacente, in festo Beati Stephani, Mar-
tyris, ab Hibernicis conburitur.

Nenagh.

*26 Decem-
ber.*

Item, obiit Domina Johanna FitzLeones, quondam
uxor Domini Simonis Genevile, sepulta in conventu Fra-
trum Predicatorum apud Trim secundo idus Aprilis.

Genevile.

Anno Domini MCCCXLVIII., et anno vicesimo secundo Regis Edwardi tertii, prima pestilentia et maxima in Hibernia que inceperat antea in aliis terris.

A.D. 1348.

Plague.

Item, isto anno, Dominus Walterus Bermyngham,
Justiciarius Hibernie, intravit Angliam et dimisit

*Bermyng-
ham.*

The brief entry on the plague in the *Annals of Ireland* by the annalist of
St Mary's Abbey, Dublin.

silence of the records signals that the Black Death did not have the effect in Dublin that it had elsewhere. However, the *Annals of Ireland* by Friar John Clyn offers a vivid eyewitness account of the Black Death's toll on the city, and other sources support this. The negative evidence afforded by archaeology speaks to the impact of the plague, which clearly disrupted the commercial life of the city. Analogy with events in other cities can also throw light on what likely happened in Dublin, as can a comparison with responses to later outbreaks of the plague in Ireland, which are more fully documented than that of 1348-1350. Of course, with each new outbreak of plague, cities adapted their responses, and, moreover, each city's experience of plague was unique. The Italian cities, for example, suffered most of all and many statements about the plague in medieval Europe are based on the extensive evidence recorded by Italian chroniclers. Nevertheless, many of the most common responses to plague transcended all national boundaries, since theories about disease and its causes were remarkably uniform; furthermore, the importance of religion in the lives of people ensured a remarkable catholicity of responses across Europe, regardless of nationality or language. Modern scientific knowledge about the plague can also throw significant light on the Black Death. Admittedly, there are important differences between modern outbreaks of plague and that in 1348. The weight of evidence would seem to suggest that the medieval pestilence was far more virulent and that therefore the accounts of devastating mortality we read of contemporary chroniclers are not to be dismissed as the mere imaginings of men with little concern for numbers and facts.

Rattus rattus, the black rat, which has been identified as the most likely host of the plague bacillus, *Y. pestis.*

PLAGUE: 'A FOUR-HANDED GAME' OR AN OPEN CASE?

The most widely accepted explanation for the cause of the Black Death has been that the bacillus *Yersinia pestis* was responsible. Following this theory, the historical demographer, Massimo Livi-Bacci, describes the plague as a game with four players: the bacillus, *Y. pestis*, which was finally identified in 1894; the black rat, *Rattus rattus*, its most common host in medieval Europe; the rat flea, *Xenopsylla cheopis*, the vector that transmits the bacillus, though the human flea, *Pulex irritans,* can also act as a vector; and man, the accidental victim.[2] The bacillus is endemic in certain kinds of rodents and especially among black rats. For reasons not fully understood, the bacilli multiply in the infected rodent's blood and then pass into the digestive system of the flea. When the rat dies, the flea deserts it and either goes into hibernation – the displaced, infectious flea can hibernate in grain or soft materrials, such as wool, for up to three months and more, and even for years in rodent burrows – or turns to another host to feed. When the supply of rats or other suitable rodents has run out, the flea turns to humans who are often the most accessible alternative hosts.

According to this theory then, the transmission of the plague bacillus to humans is an anomaly in that plague is a zoonose, a disease of rodents and their fleas, and humans enter the cycle only by chance: 'the plague is only a sideshow to what the *Y. pestis* is really doing', as one scientist has recently written.[3] The bacillus is transmitted to humans either by a flea bite, or by direct contact through a break in the skin, or by respiratory means. There is some evidence that it can also be transmitted by eating infected substances, such as infected wild animals, but this theory is not universally accepted. Swellings or buboes usually, though not necessarily, then appear on the lymph nodes, followed in severe cases by fever and coma. Case mortality is between $\frac{2}{3}$ and $\frac{4}{5}$ for the bubonic form of the plague, though in its pneumonic form plague is among the most deadly of diseases and has an almost 100% mortality rate. However, plague can present in a wide variety of forms, ranging from the mild to the most severe, and modern epidemics have been observed to differ widely in their severity. The outbreak of the Black Death was among the most severe recorded and has therefore attracted all the more attention.

Recent debates among bacteriologists and biological anthropologists about the nature of the pathogen causing the Black Death have raised many questions and doubts about what has until now been considered a closed case. In particular, scientists have for long been troubled by features of the

Victim of plague, with the bubo characteristic
of the bubonic form of the disease.

medieval plague that do not accord with observations gleaned
from nineteenth and twentieth-century outbreaks of bubonic
plague. Questions have been raised about the failure of
medieval chroniclers to include any reports of dead rats, such
as these which preceded modern outbreaks of the disease
among humans. Even centuries before, Avicenna had noticed
the strange behaviour of rats on the approach of plague and,
in the *Bhagavata Purana*, people were advised to leave their
houses when they saw unusual mortality among rats.[4] During
1347-1350, however, no such observations were recorded.
Other characteristics of the medieval epidemic, such as its
rapid spread and its high mortality, are in sharp contrast to the
low mortality rate and slow pace of modern outbreaks of

Yersinial plague. Some commentators have therefore called into question the nature of the evidence from medieval sources, suggesting it is exaggerated hearsay. Others have suggested that the Black Death must have been caused not by bubonic plague but by some other disease. The historian S.K. Cohn in *The Black Death Transformed* argues that whatever disease may have been responsible for the medieval epidemic, it was not bubonic plague and that the epidemiology of the modern plague has uncritically been imposed on the medieval plague. In their *Biology of Plagues: Evidence from Historical Populations*, S. Scott and C.J. Duncan claim that the Black Death was not an outbreak of bubonic plague but a form of haemorrhagic viral disease, perhaps similar to the Ebola virus. Dr Graham Twigg in *The Black Death: A Biological Reappraisal* claims that it was more likely an outbreak of pulmonary anthrax, not of bubonic plague.

However, a recent study in France in 2000 claims to offer definitive molecular evidence that *Y. pestis* was indeed the cause of the Black Death. Researchers examined the dental pulp in the corpses of three presumed victims of the Black Death that had been discovered in a mass grave in Montpellier, and identified the DNA sequence as being identical to that of modern *Y. pestis*. On the basis of their findings, they confidently concluded, 'we believe that we can end the controversy: medieval Black Death was plague'.[5] However, the question of the precise identity of the bacillus was reopened in 2002 when a group of biological anthropologists concluded, primarily on the basis of their examination of English historical records, that the modern *Y. pestis* was unlikely to have been the cause of the Black Death. Rather, they hypothesised, the causative pathogen was either an ancestor of *Y. pestis*, is now extinct or has evolved beyond recognition.[6] The debate goes on, and definitive conclusions have yet to be reached. Perhaps further scientific study will yield final conclusive answers as to the precise nature of the disease that devastated Europe in the Middle Ages. In the meantime, the debate has important implications for considerations of the human experience of the plague. In particular, the observations of contemporary chroniclers regarding the highly contagious nature of the epidemic, its rapid transmission and the huge numbers of people it killed are now increasingly being accepted as valid, where formerly they were dismissed as apocalyptic metaphors or the fabrications of innumerate men. There is also convincing evidence that the pneumonic strain of the plague, which is far more lethal than the bubonic strain and does not rely on rats and fleas for its dissemination, dominated in the early stages of the Black Death epidemic.

Many questions also remain about the role played by the human factor in the dissemination of the Black Death. Some epidemiologists, accepting that the Black Death was an outbreak of bubonic plague, argue that diseases spread by animals, like bubonic plague, have little to do with human behaviour and depend solely on exogenous factors such as climate and rodent life patterns. According to this view, the Black Death spread completely independently of the human environment. Livi-Bacci puts the position unambiguously:

> The ability of the plague to infect and kill bore no relation to one's state of health, age, or level of nutrition. It struck urban and rural populations with equal violence, and with the exception of a few isolated areas, density levels presented no obstacle to its spread.[7]

This theory is borne out by those recent studies claiming that *Y. pestis*, at least in its modern form, was not the causative agent of the Black Death. If this hypothesis is correct, then it is very likely that the epidemic spread through person-to-person contact, and did not depend on the prior infection of rats, and by implication, on rat and population density. On the other hand, if the modern *Y. pestis* was the causative agent, then in considering its diffusion a number of factors are crucial: the size and density of the rat population, the size and mobility of the flea population, the density and vulnerability of the human population and, above all, patterns of mobility and communication. Interaction between rat and man, or flea and man, must also be close for transmission to occur.

The human factor is also of some significance in explaining the high levels of mortality. Included here are the extent of people's exposure to infection, their resistance, and the virulence and frequency of the pathogen. Each of these is in turn influenced by further considerations. The extent of exposure is affected by population density, public health, sanitation and living standards; resistance can be influenced by nutrition levels, by immunity either natural or acquired, and by medical knowledge; and finally, climate as well as other biological and zoological factors affect the virulence and frequency of the pathogen. Clearly the higher mortality in cities and towns can be attributed partly at least to the fact that more people lived there. Some argue that the lack of sanitation in cities contributed to greater morbidity and point to the fact that improved public health in later centuries was crucial in bringing about the disappearance of plague in Europe. Others argue that sanitary measures are effective only against water and food-borne micro-organisms such as in cholera.[8] Less clear are the climatic conditions required. The rat flea, *X. cheopis*, needs temperatures between 15°C and 25°C and high humidity, about 90 to 95%, in order to survive. *Y. pestis* itself is extremely sensitive to sunlight and cannot survive long in hot, dry weather. Cold weather tends to check the spread of plague, unless it has segued into a pneumonic form, which appears only in cold climates or in wintertime and is transmitted directly by respiratory means.

THE TRANSMISSION OF PLAGUE: EXPOSURE

Trading Links and Communications

One facet of the history of the Black Death in Europe that remains undisputed so far is the path of its dissemination throughout the Continent. It originated in the East and spread quickly from country to country along the routes that had opened up Europe to the East in the eleventh century. If the causative pathogen was *Y. pestis*, then it was carried by the black rat, which was to be found primarily in large cities, especially ports, and which thrives in dry surroundings such as grain depots and in the holds of ships. Because the black rat itself is very sedentary and rarely travels outside a limited radius, the bacillus is usually transmitted over wide areas by the passive transport of the rat and flea. Ships carrying grain or cloth brought infected rats into the ports of Europe, and infected fleas most likely travelled in the merchandise of merchants and mariners. Alternatively, if the epidemic was caused by some other pathogen, then it was most likely carried by merchants and travellers and transmitted by direct contact.

Death and the Sailor by Hans Holbein.

The plague in Ireland originated in Dublin and Drogheda, and perhaps in some towns and cities along the south and south-eastern coasts. By the fourteenth century, Dublin had become a common destination for merchants from all over Europe, and in the process part of the same disease pool. Though it was not necessarily the busiest port in Ireland, with New Ross and Drogheda vying for that position, nevertheless its proximity to ports on the West Coast of England meant that it was an important centre for trade, particularly in grain. Contemporary documents and pottery records indicate trading connections with La Rochelle, Aquitaine, Bordeaux, Rouen, Dieppe, Flanders, Glasgow, Chester,

Liverpool and above all Bristol. With favourable winds, a boat could sail 100 miles a day; a trip from London to Avignon took some two weeks, and from Dublin a few days longer. Given such trading connections, plague could travel quite quickly either from England or from mainland Europe. As elsewhere throughout Europe then, the epidemic very likely was brought to Ireland either by rats lodged in the holds of ships plying between Dublin and Bristol, Chester or Bordeaux, or by fleas lodged in the merchandise of merchants and sailors or even on the merchants themselves.

That the plague reached Dublin by sea is most likely since overland access to the city was not easy. Trade with the hinterland was often conducted along the River Liffey, which was used for the transport of provisions. There were long-distance routes or *slíghe* connecting Dublin with Cork, Waterford, Limerick, Galway and to the north, with Tara and Derry. How easily these roads could be traversed is a matter of question. Jean Creton, a French visitor who accompanied Richard II to Ireland in 1399, wrote that there were no roads in Ireland and bogs so deep one could disappear in them. Under normal conditions however, a typical day's journey overland at this time would be about 20 miles a day on foot, though that could rise to 30 or 35 miles a day if on horseback. Travelling was frequent: to markets and fairs, to far-flung estates, to sites of pilgrimage. However, access to Dublin was rendered particularly difficult in the mid-fourteenth century, thanks principally to the resurgent power of the Gaelic chieftains in Wicklow. A contemporary account describes the city as 'situated in a more remote part of that land', far from the richer manors in the south-east. The result was that merchants dared not trade in County Kilkenny, and public officials could not easily travel to Dublin to render their accounts at the exchequer.[9]

Within the city itself, there was plenty of human traffic, facilitating the rapid diffusion of plague. The streets were busy places: butchers and craftsmen carried out their business in the open. Selling was done from benches in the doorways where people would congregate, or in the market places where larger crowds gathered. Weekly markets and annual fairs were common; the most famous fair, that at Donnybrook, had been established in 1204, initially for eight days annually, and extended in 1214 to fifteen days. Pilgrims were a common sight, and the shrines at Christ Church Cathedral in particular were popular places of pilgrimage. Moreover, Dublin would seem to have been replete with vagrants and beggars who were seen as transmitters of plague even in the early thirteenth century when the oath of office of the city provost included the undertaking that he would '...banish all beggars in time of sickness and plague'.[10] Together, these conditions would also allow for a high density of rats and fleas and for the rapid transmission of any kind of infectious pathogen.

Density of Population

A high population density clearly creates the kind of living conditions that can facilitate the propagation of fleas and rats and significantly affects the speed with which most epidemics are transmitted. Scientists have not been able to determine the minimum density necessary for an epidemic to develop, but undoubtedly many medieval towns provided the ideal conditions. With the growing population of medieval cities in the thirteenth and early fourteenth centuries, the pest population, whether of rats or fleas, would have grown apace. Of course, medieval Dublin was not as heavily populated a city as some other contemporary Italian or French cities; Irish society was still rural, and its cities were not yet the centres of population they were to become in later centuries. Dublin, while one of the larger towns of Ireland, was yet but one among many, and other towns such as New Ross and Drogheda vied with it for size.

Nevertheless with an estimated 44 acres enclosed within its walls, the city would not have been sparsely populated. Speed's Map of Dublin (see Plate 3) shows a compact, walled town with sizeable suburbs to the north, south and west of the city. Though the medieval city had expanded rapidly in the twelfth and thirteenth centuries, it was still circumscribed by its walls and by the River Poddle. The possibilities of expansion were further limited at this time because of the dangers posed by the Gaelic-Irish, who controlled areas to the south of the city. Consequently, settlement within the city was quite concentrated, centered on the area around Christ Church Cathedral where most archaeological explorations have been carried out. But the population was pushing those limits. Houses were even built on the city walls, and throughout the Middle Ages the city leased space on the walls for the building of houses. The density of the population is further underlined by the large number of churches in the city, with at least twenty-four churches and religious houses both within and without the walls. Moreover, the layout of the city's streets further facilitated rapid transmission. The streets did not follow a regular plan, and the city was very likely a jumble of buildings. Dr G. Twigg, in questioning the bubonic plague diagnosis of the Black Death, argued that plague could not have spread in medieval cities as quickly as the chroniclers described because the typical medieval city was built on a grid plan and because studies in similar grid plan North-

American cities have shown that rats do not move from the block in which they were born. However, recent topographical studies of Dublin indicate that its layout at least was highly irregular and did not follow a comprehensive system.[11]

Furthermore, there was also considerable settlement in suburbs outside the walls, with an estimated 80% of the population living in clusters that had grown up around a number of ecclesiastical sites. These included St Mary's Abbey, St Michan's Church and the Dominican Priory of St Saviour to the north, the Hospital of St John the Baptist and the Abbey of St Thomas to the west, St Patrick's Cathedral to the south and the Augustinian Priory of All Hallows to the east. A number of these were large landowners: St Mary's Abbey held about 17,125 acres, Christ Church 10,538, and the Priory and Hospital of St John the Baptist owned approximately 12,690 acres both in Dublin and in other parts of the country. The suburbs that grew up, however, remained outside the walls, unlike Continental cities where new walls were built to incorporate the expanding suburbs. The reason for this was partly that the system of land tenure allowed the ecclesiastical authorities to retain control of large areas. These abbeys and monasteries acted as developers in the suburbs, granting and leasing plots, establishing markets and parishes and attracting tenants. The population density then, both within the walls and in the suburbs, would certainly have been adequate to support a sizeable rat and flea population and to enable epidemics to spread rapidly.[12]

Quite how crowded Dublin was in the mid-fourteenth century is a much-debated subject however, and estimates of its population vary greatly. The population of medieval cities everywhere had expanded alongside the general population increase from between c.1100 to 1300, and suffered a setback with the Black Death and subsequent outbreaks in the later fourteenth century, only to recover sometime in the sixteenth century. Dublin followed a similar pattern, though we have little evidence for the actual size of its population at any stage throughout this process. The documented expansion of the city in the thirteenth century, while partly a response to an increase in population, could also have been partly undertaken in anticipation of continuing increases, as was the case in cities elsewhere in Europe. But precise calculations of its pre-plague population are not possible, though many have attempted estimates. One very low estimate put the population at 3,500 in the early fourteenth century. The historical demographer, J.C. Russell, estimated that the population of Dublin in the mid-thirteenth century was about 10,000, calculating about 100-120 persons for each of the 112 hectares he surmised for the city's area. Dr B.J. Graham has argued that this figure is exaggerated as the area of the walled town was only about 18 hectares, while granting that some of the population lived outside the walls. T.H. Hollingsworth, on the other hand, considered Russell's estimates too low. Using evidence of guild membership, a household multiplier of four to account for the dependents of each guild member, and adding some 6,000 for clergy, soldiers and other non-guild members, Hollingsworth very tentatively guessed its population in 1246 to be closer to 20,000 and in 1280 to be about 25,000. This figure he considered to be a reasonable guess, particularly by comparison with the 57,000 people he estimated for London at the same time. Dr G. MacNiocaill, calculating on the basis of the average number of admissions to the franchise and using the same household multiplier of four, agrees with

Hollingsworth's figure of about 20,000 for the mid-thirteenth century. Using similar calculations, he suggests Dublin's population in 1476 could have dropped as low as 6,000. But, he adds:

> …this is the merest guesswork, since Hollingsworth's estimate depends on applying multipliers of assumed family size – of which we know nothing, except that it was unlikely to be uniform – to an estimate of the numbers of guild members with the degree of plausibility and probability dropping sharply at each step.[13]

More recent demographers argue that a household multiplier of four is far too low for the average household in the medieval city, which in general tended to be much larger than the typical rural household. Urban households often included as many as seven or eight people and Gilbert li Muisis in his chronicle of Tournai, for example even notes households of ten and more. If a household multiplier of eight were used, Hollingsworth's and MacNiocaill's estimates would increase to well over 30,000. Dr T. Barry, using the mortality figures offered by Friar Clyn for the Black Death in Dublin and an average mortality rate of 33%, entertains a figure of around 42,000 inhabitants in the mid-fourteenth century, a figure which, if correct, would indicate the city's limits must have extended much further than is presently judged. Other estimates, based on Clyn's figures for Black Death mortality, have guessed population figures of 35,000 and 28,000, depending on the average mortality rate that is used in the calculation.[14]

The population of other cities can be a guide to Dublin's probable size. In Italy, one of the most populous regions in medieval Europe, Milan, Florence and Venice each had about 100,000 inhabitants; Genoa, Rome and Bologna had between 50,000 and 75,000; Cremona, Padua and others had populations between 10,000 and 50,000; over 150 other towns had between 2,000 and 10,000. Paris by the mid-fourteenth century had a population close to 100,000; Toulouse about 25,000; Rouen and Bordeaux had about 10,000; then another fifty towns had a few thousand people. In Germany the largest town was Cologne with about 50,000, while about fifty towns had populations over 2,000. London had about 60,000, York and Bristol about 15,000. By far the greatest number of towns in England had between 500 and 6,000. However, recent demographic studies have tended to revise upwards the population of English cities. London's population, for example, which used to be estimated at around 50,000 inhabitants in 1300 is now estimated at between 80-100,000 in 1300; and the population of Norwich has been upgraded from 10,000 to 42,000 and even higher.[15]

All this suggests that likely quite a large population was crowded within the walls of Dublin and in the suburbs outside the walls, whose further expansion was checked by geographical and political factors. The result was a densely populated city, where people lived in close contact with one another, with all the accompanying consequences for public health.

Public Health and Sanitation
The conditions in which people lived in these towns provided the perfect incubator for nurturing fleas and rats and

facilitated the transmission of epidemics. Towns, and especially coastal trading towns, are the natural habitat for the black rat whose preferred habitation is a warm place such as a warehouse, with a temperature of 38.09°C. Fleas lodged in the merchandise of the ships and warehouses. Dublin's port provided these conditions, as did the town itself, which was similar to many other European cities at this time. Streets were made of packed earth or mud, full of ruts and holes, though some streets had been paved by 1348 – street paving had begun in Dublin in 1329, earlier than in other cities, such as Bristol, where streets weren't paved until 1488. Drains ran in the middle of the roads. Butchers killed animals on the streets and deposited their remains on the city's streets or in the river. Complaints were constant about the dumping of waste, both in public places and in rivers, as well as about contaminated water supplies and noxious smells. Pigs roamed freely, mainly because almost every household kept them, and foraged among the waste dumped outside the houses. The city's authorities made repeated efforts to forbid them within the city's walls, to require licences for ownership and to fine unlicensed owners, but the repetition of the ordinances suggests limited success.[16]

Moreover, sanitary facilities in the city were extremely inadequate and public hygiene measures a hit-and-miss affair. Generally, each homeowner was expected to cleanse the area in front of his or her own house, but clearly enforcement was a problem. A request from around 1317 from the citizens of Dublin asked that the city be cleansed twice weekly. Records from other cities provide further details of typical public sanitation. The city authorities of Kilkenny, for example, decreed in 1337 that:

If anyone be found washing clothing or the intestines of animals or anything else in the fountains of the said town they shall be forfeited and if anyone be found committing any other enormity in the said fountains he shall be put in the tumbrel.

The houses of the wealthier citizens probably had private latrines and these, as elsewhere in Europe, were often built over a river or running water. An example of sanitary arrangements is provided by an agreement made in 1317 between the city's authorities and John de Grauntsete, one of Dublin's wealthier citizens, and his wife. The mayor granted approval for a latrine, which the de Grauntsetes had built, that drained through an opening in the wall 'into the waters of Anna Liffey'. In return the de Grauntsetes promised to pay an annual rent of twelve pence and accepted that if the rent fell into arrears the city had the right to enforce payment by obstructing the latrine, an effective way of cutting off services! Not surprisingly in view of such arrangements, the water supply was always contaminated by waste. For other citizens, there were undoubtedly some public latrines, though most likely the street served frequently as such.[17]

Uncovered drains ran above ground along the sides of houses, carrying rainwater and sewage to the river or to cesspits in open areas beyond. These drains were lined with planks of wood and were later replaced by stone drains. Wood-lined cesspits were found during archaeological investigations at Winetavern Street, at Christchurch Place and Wood Quay.[18] However, with the rapid growth of the city in the thirteenth century, these must have been totally inadequate, and would have contributed in no small measure to the smells that contemporaries considered as one of the sources of epidemics. Moreover, these cesspits and wooden drains provided suitable habitations for rats and facilitated their propagation.

Whether public hygiene deficiencies contributed to the 1348 epidemic is a matter of question. If the outbreak was of bubonic plague, then deficiencies in public hygiene would not have caused the bacillus to emerge, but would have affected its transmission and people's exposure to it. If some pathogen other than *Y. pestis* was the cause, then public health conditions could have been significant. In the fourteenth century however, the authorities were clearly convinced that public health measures were crucial in fighting disease. In line with the best medical theory of the time, pestilence was associated with foul air and most public sanitation measures related to cleansing the air and dealing with the root causes of foul air. The belief was that bad air was the medium through which disease was disseminated and that 'seeds' of disease attached themselves to clothing, animals and places. In fact, the so-called miasmatic theory persisted until well into the nineteenth century when it was superseded by germ theory. It was a theory that was logically worked out in the best medieval fashion. Medical authorities generally agreed that the pestilence originated in a prime cause, the wrath of God, which caused planetary disturbances or harmful planetary conjunctions that led to disruptions in the air. The Masters of the Medical Faculty of the Sorbonne in Paris, for example, surmised that the conjunction of Saturn, Mars and Jupiter in Aquarius on 20 March 1345 at 1.00 p.m. was, 'along with other conjunctions and eclipses', the remote cause of a 'deadly corruption of the surrounding air', which brought mortality and famine. This type of explanation was not new and had a respectable ancestry. Albertus Magnus, commenting on a pseudo-Aristotelian work, the *De Causis Proprietatum Elementorum*, wrote that the conjunction of Mars and Jupiter provokes:

> a great pestilence in the air, particularly when it happens in a warm and humid sign of the zodiac... This was the result of the combined effect of the actions of both planets since Jupiter, a warm and humid planet, elevates bad vapours from earth and water, while Mars, an intemperately warm and dry planet, ignites the elevated vapours thus causing the multiplication in the air of lightnings, sparks, pestiferous vapours and fires.

The theory then ran that as a result of the planetary movements, pestilential vapours arose from the earth (due to animal dung, putrefying corpses, etc.) and spread, carried especially by southern winds which were seen as the pre-eminent plague winds. Alternatively, corrupt air could also arise from below the surface of the earth, which had been disturbed by earthquakes and floods.[19]

It is not surprising then that given this understanding of the cause of plague and its transmission, the noxious smells from cesspits, rubbish heaps and rubbish-strewn streets should have for so long troubled urban authorities throughout Europe. In general, from the turn of the fourteenth century contaminated air is increasingly mentioned in the public records as being the cause of disease, and the particular sources cited are rotting animal corpses, manure heaps, the tanning of hides within the town and the slaughter of cattle. Dublin in

1336 was described as pervaded by 'excessive and noxious stenches' emanating from the butchering of cattle. Complaints continued into the fifteenth century, such as the following:

Dung heaps, swine, hog sties and other nuisances in the streets, lanes and suburbs of Dublin infect the air and produce mortality, fevers and pestilence throughout that city.[20]

Dublin was not unique in this. Even a great city like London suffered too from smells, dung heaps, wandering swine and pigsties. A law passed in London in the time of Edward I ordained that '…he who shall wish to feed a pig, must feed it in his house' and that any swine found wandering would be forfeited. In 1348 yet more sanitary ordinances were passed but to little effect, as in 1361 the King issued a further proclamation that all cattle and pigs were to be killed outside the city:

Because by killing of great beasts, from whose putrid blood running down the streets and the bowels cast into the Thames, the air in the city is very much corrupted and infected, whence abominable and most filthy stinks proceed, sicknesses and many other evils have happened…

While complaints about such conditions were chronic, the outbreak of disease spurred more urgent action. When plague broke out, not only was pestilential or corrupt air blamed, so too was everything associated with disease and dirt. In Dublin, regulations were enacted governing the placement of latrines and hogs' sties, but the pig problem was not to be solved for many centuries.[21]

Housing

The unhygienic conditions without were completed by conditions within people's houses. Much of the extant evidence about housing in medieval Dublin comes from excavations at Wood Quay and High Street.[22] Most medieval houses were timber-framed with wattle and daub walls, roofs were of thatch, sometimes covered with plaster or boards, and many were lined with a layer of lead to reduce the risk of fire. In any case, the materials used for building were soft for the most part, thereby providing rats and fleas with easy access to houses. Though stone was increasingly used in the late thirteenth and fourteenth centuries, stone houses would still have been the exception rather than the rule; even as late as 1597, Winetavern Street is recorded as having both 'stone mansions and wooden houses'. The few stone dwellings extant in 1348 would have belonged to wealthier citizens. One such was the archbishop's manor house at Swords in County Dublin, described thus in 1326:

> There was a hall, a chamber for the archbishop annexed to it, of which the walls are stone and crenellated like a castle and roofed with shingles; and there is a kitchen there with a larder, whose walls are stone and roof of shingle, a chapel with stone walls and shingle roof... near the gate is a chamber for the constable and four chambers for knights, squires, roofed with shingles; under these, a stable and bakehouse; there was a house for a dairy and carpentry... [23]

If the Black Death was in fact an outbreak of bubonic plague, then the stone houses of Dublin's wealthy were an important factor in protecting them from the inroads of rats and therefore the worst ravages of the plague, just as in England where the nobility were hardly affected by plague. On the other hand, the wooden houses of the poor would have offered little protection.

Conditions within the houses, especially of the poor, facilitated the transmission and reception of disease. People lived in very close quarters, often with their animals – and especially pigs – sharing the living quarters. Studies of modern plague outbreaks in India and China have shown that badly ventilated, crowded buildings as well as cold weather were important factors in diffusing plague, and furthermore contributed to the outbreak of the pneumonic form of plague, which is far more virulent and spreads rapidly by direct transmission.[24] The average house in cities such as Dublin in the Middle Ages was not significantly different from dwellings in India in the nineteenth century. The typical house offered little ventilation and was single-storeyed, with at most two or three rooms, a living area, kitchen and a communal bedroom, in which households of at least five, and perhaps up to ten or twelve, as well as a number of animals lived. Some eleventh and twelfth-century houses were unearthed in Dublin, which were about 7 x 4 metres, with open hearths in the centre and bedding of brushwood along the walls. Inside floors were strewn with fermenting straw and rushes which, analysis has shown, sheltered many fleas and all sorts of insects, and which may have been deliberately conceived as a form of heating. Though the houses excavated were largely eleventh-century, conditions had not changed significantly by the mid-fourteenth century. Even some 150 years later, Erasmus described similar conditions in houses in England:

Almost all the floors are clay and rushes from the marshes, so carelessly renewed that the foundation sometimes remains for twenty years, harbouring there below spittle and vomit and urine of dogs and men, beer that hath been cast forth and remnants of fishes and other filth unnameable.

Not everybody lived in houses, however. The city's large and notorious population of beggars and vagrants lived on the streets and alleys. Jean Creton, who travelled to Ireland in 1399, described Waterford as a city where 'the wretched and filthy people, some in rags, others girt with a rope, had the one a hole, the other a hut for their dwelling'. Dublin would have afforded similar accommodation to its vagrants.[25]

Resistance to Infection

Contemporaries thought of disease in terms of 'seed and soil': disease required not only a source, but also a human breeding ground vulnerable to its inroads. Here many factors played a part, and why some areas and cities escaped plague while others were devastated is an issue that has exercised many epidemiologists and historians. Theories abound, particularly about the issue of immunity, but there is little consensus, not surprising given that so little still is known about the determinants of resistance to disease. The typical medieval town dweller was prey to all sorts of health hazards that contributed to a general weakening of immunological health. Immunity from disease in general is affected by many factors: prior exposure, which may lead to acquired immunity, and the overall health of the individual, which affects innate immunity. There is no general agreement on the subject of acquired immunity. Some argue that sections of the population or people in certain areas may have acquired genetic protection from Justinian's Plague in the sixth century; others argue that over time people developed immunity. Whether immunity to plague is even possible is a much-debated issue. Recent theories proposing that the Black Death was caused not by bubonic plague but by some other disease allow for the possibility of acquired immunity. However, this factor is perhaps of more significance in the plague outbreaks of the later fourteenth, fifteenth and sixteenth centuries than it would have been in 1348 when Europe was faced with a hitherto unknown disease.[26]

Innate immunity depends on the health of the individual, which is influenced by nutrition, living conditions and socioeconomic status. Each of these factors is the subject of much dissent, particularly nutrition. Massimo Livi-Bacci asserts that 'nourishment emerges as a powerful factor of constraint in the history of European population, at least up until the nineteenth century'. But the connection between nutrition levels and susceptibility to plague is not so clear-cut. In general, malnutrition is connected in complex ways with lower fertility and higher mortality levels, though epidemiologists are not unanimous on the precise details. Food shortages affect the immune systems of children in particular, increasing their susceptibility to disease, and severe malnutrition can prevent the proper biological development of their immune systems. Some argue that malnutrition of the sort to be expected from the monoculture of medieval agriculture causes anaemia in the population at large and lowers resistance to infectious disease:

Prolonged malnutrition heightens the chances of epidemics breaking out, infectious diseases take a heavier toll. This is the explanation of the havoc wrought by the Black Death and other epidemics of the fourteenth century.[27]

In his *Treatise on Plague*, which draws on extensive contemporary reports of plague in late nineteenth and early twentieth-century India, China and Egypt, W.J. Simpson asserted that famine and malnutrition increased the susceptibility of populations to plague. Other studies, while granting a connection between malnutrition or hunger and vulnerability to disease, contend that plague is one of the infectious bacterial diseases that is only slightly influenced by a person's nutritional status. Yet others argue that malnutrition can actually help protect against disease by depriving the hostile microorganisms of nutrients. In general, writes Livi-Bacci, there is some evidence that:

> nutritional deficiencies, if they can depress the human body's defences, can also in certain cases interfere with the metabolic and reproductive process of the attacking micro-organism. In some cases malnutrition has an antagonistic, rather than a synergic, effect, thus limiting the damage done by infection.[28]

Nevertheless, he adds, the link between nutritional deficiency and plague mortality appears minimal or non-existent and malnutrition had little or no impact on the outbreak or the effects of plague. However, definitive conclusions about the role of nutrition are not possible in view of the questions that have been raised about the nature of the bacillus that caused the Black Death. Clearly, the factors that influence mortality in modern outbreaks of plague cannot unreservedly be attributed to the medieval epidemic, since it clearly was so much more virulent than modern outbreaks of *Y. pestis*.

Compelling, if inconclusive, arguments have been made that prior famines had an effect on the mortality caused by the Black Death. Dr W. Jordan, in his study *The Great Famine*, posits the hypothesis that at the time of the Black Death, those adults who had been young children during the famine years of 1315-1318 were more susceptible to the plague than those who had been adults during the famine or who had grown up earlier or later, in more prosperous times. Food shortages are known to increase children's susceptibility to disease since low body weight increases susceptibility to diarrhoea, which in turn gradually undermines resistance to infection. Thus, Jordan argues, those who experienced famine in childhood grew up to have nutritionally-induced immune problems, which may have contributed to the high plague mortality thirty years later. This theory seems to be supported by the relatively low plague mortality rates in areas like Flanders. There the famine of 1315-1318 had claimed large numbers of children, so that those who were adults during the plague years would have been born after the famine and therefore would have been more able to resist it. Records from some well-documented manors in England would also seem to support this theory: at Halesowen manor, near Birmingham, for example, mortality from the outbreak of 1348 was highest in the thirty to fifty-nine age group – that is the group that would have been children in 1315, whereas those under twenty were hardly affected.[29]

Starvation-induced cannibalism.

As the famine of 1315-1318 had been particularly devastating in Dublin and its surroundings, this is a possible, albeit non-quantifiable, factor in considering plague mortality in Dublin.

While the effect of malnutrition on plague remains in question, there is no doubt that the intermittent food shortages and the consequent malnutrition of many clearly added considerably to the distress of medieval townspeople and meant that they were not in a position to recover quickly from outbreaks of disease. Because the food supply in Dublin was so dependent on what could be supplied locally, it was often disrupted by political changes, military campaigns and poor harvests. Famines were particularly frequent from the end of the thirteenth century, partly due to climate change, partly to war. All the annals record a famine in 1271 both in Dublin and throughout the country, which was so severe 'that multitudes of poor people died of cold and hunger and the rich suffered hardship'. In 1294 a 'great famine and pestilence' is recorded throughout Ireland that continued for the following two years and Clyn notes that many perished from the hunger; a record from Christ Church Cathedral records that the famine was so great that people ate the corpses of those who had been hanged at the crossroads.[30] A few years later, in 1310, the annalist of St Mary's Abbey wrote of a great shortage of wheat throughout the country and that concerns about the food supply in Dublin were so acute that the city's bakers were dragged through the streets as punishment for using false weights. The great famine of 1317 was so severe in the city that many died of hunger, especially among the poor, while others were reduced to begging. Reports of cannibalism were rife and, according to the same annalist, the soldiers in the Ulster Army of the Bruces were 'so destroyed with hunger' that they dug up the bodies of the dead from the cemeteries and consumed them, and mothers ate their own children. In 1331 he reported a great famine in the city, which ended when a school of whales, called 'Thurlhedis' or 'turlhydes,' was washed up at the mouth of the Dodder and divided out among the citizens. The event was commemorated by James Joyce centuries later:

A school of turlehide whales stranded in hot noon, spouting, hobbling in the shallows. Then from the starving cagework city a horde of jerkined dwarfs, my people, with flayers' knives, running, scaling, hacking in green blubbery whalemeat. Famine, plague and slaughters.[31]

Whatever the precise accuracy of such stories, they do indicate that the food supply could never be taken for granted. As the fourteenth century progressed, and with the increasing warfare in Leinster, Dublin's reserves of grain were further depleted by the supplies they were required to give to the armies sent to curb the chieftains of Leinster, and to the King's armies in France and Scotland. For example, in 1316 the mayor and bailiffs of Dublin were ordered to provide ale, wheat and flour for the 300 armed men granted them in aid of the King's war against the Irish in the Wicklow mountains.[32]

Offsetting this chronic shortage of food is the possibility that because of Dublin's proximity to fishing grounds and the countryside, the quality of nutrition in the city was better, at least for some of its citizens, than was the case in some other European cities. Archaeologists have uncovered traces of a wide variety of foods traded in the markets, which give a good idea of what some medieval Dubliners ate: cockles and mussels, oysters, fruits such as strawberries, apples, pears, cherries, plums, sloes, blackberries, bilberries, rowan berries and hazel nuts – obviously the produce of the surrounding countryside – as well as oysters and shellfish. However, there would have been a stark contrast between the diet of the wealthy and that of the poor. The poor had a subsistence diet, relying mainly on grain, so that grain shortages would have fallen particularly hard on them. Excavations have also shown that they ate a kind of bread or porridge made from goosefoot (*Chenopodium album*) and knotgrass (*Polygonum*), along with other weeds such as black bindweed and pale persicaria.[33] They couldn't afford to eat more expensive food: a washerwoman at this time was paid six pence for half a year's work, a carpenter earned two pence a day, whereas a typical dinner during Lent in the priory of Holy Trinity cost three shillings or thirty-six pence. The wealthy enjoyed a higher standard of nutrition. Records from Holy Trinity Priory, for example, indicate that wine was a regular accompaniment to dinners of fowl, lamb, beef, mutton, pork, pigeons, goslings, rabbits, larks and plovers. An early fourteenth-century poem by Friar Michael of Kildare, 'The Land of Cokaygne' indicates, with some satirical exaggeration, what may have been common fare for the monks of St Mary's Abbey:

> *Here there is a right fair abbey*
> *Both of white monks and of grey.*
> *Here are bowers and high halls,*
> *And of pasties are the walls*
> *Of flesh and fish and of rich meat,*
> *All the best that men may eat.*
>
> *Flour-cakes, the shingles all*
> *Of church and cloister, bower and hall,*
> *Pins there are of puddings rich,*
> *Meat that princes can bewitch.*
> *Men may sit and eat it long*
> *All with right and not with wrong.*[34]

Yet, notwithstanding this nutritional discrepancy, better nutrition did not necessarily guarantee a longer life for the upper classes and did not seem to protect them to any significant degree against epidemics. In fact, until the early modern age, life expectancy was about the same for both rich and poor – in general between twenty-five and thirty-five years of age. For generations born in Europe between 1350 and

1500, all classes had a life expectancy of twenty-six years. In England too, according to the historical demographer, J.C. Russell, life expectancy at birth for those born between 1276-1300 was 31.3 years; in 1301-1325 it was 29.8 and in 1326-1350 it was 27.2. Even for English ducal families born between 1330 and 1479, life expectancy at birth was about twenty-two years, or thirty-one years if deaths from violent causes are excluded. Conditions in Ireland would have been similar. Excavations in Cork indicate what was probably common in Irish towns at the time: of the 216 skeletons examined, 24% died before their early twenties and 36.5% died in the twenty to thirty age group. Only 1.8% survived beyond fifty years; 48.1% were aged between sixteen and early twenties and the largest group were between six and ten years old. The cause of death could not be ascertained in most cases, though the individuals there were found to have suffered from an array of ailments including degenerative joint disease, osteoarthritis, dental disease as well as traumas caused by injury.[35]

Finally, the typical medieval town dweller was prey to all sorts of other health risks: anthrax, diphtheria, dysentery, gonorrhoea, influenza, leprosy, pneumonia, scabies, scurvy, smallpox, tuberculosis and typhoid fever are but a few of the diseases that were common. While not directly linked to bubonic plague, these undoubtedly contributed to a general weakening of immunological health. Of course, as long as the precise bacteriological cause of the Black Death remains in question, so do issues relating to immunity and the role of nutrition.

The outbreak of plague was associated with various ecological disasters, such as earthquakes, and with unusual events, such as the appearance of comets or plagues of locusts.

Virulence of Yersinia pestis

The virulence of the Black Death is one of the features most emphasised by medieval chroniclers and most debated by modern researchers. No doubt the fact that Europe in 1348 was virgin territory contributed to its virulence. There is considerable evidence that the medieval plague was more morbid than later outbreaks, due perhaps to genetic changes in the bacillus. Whether this means that the bacillus was something other than *Y. pestis* remains to be decided.

A long-debated theory links the plague to environmental factors. One of the traditional explanations for its outbreak has been that ecological changes in central Asia at this time, caused perhaps by earthquakes, displaced infected rodents and drove them into closer contact with the human population. In 1349, the English chronicler Knighton reported earthquakes at Corinth and in Achaea, Cyprus and Italy that levelled mountains in Cyprus and destroyed many villages and cities, including Naples.[36] Other contemporaries reported unheard-of tempests, showers of frogs, scorpions and venomous beasts, hailstones so large as to be fatal, and fire from the heavens that burned up cities in the East. Such reports have often been interpreted as merely apocalyptic with little connection to historical fact. However, theories regarding the link between ecological changes and epidemics persist. The outbreak of bubonic plague in twentieth-century San Francisco, for example, was also associated with an earthquake.

That the virulence of the Black Death may be connected with meteorological factors is also a recurrent theory among epidemiologists and a significant body of recent research has focused on the influence of climatic factors in determining outbreaks of plague. In Northwestern Europe, later outbreaks of urban plagues were associated with cold winters, dry springs and hot, dry summers (plus good harvests). Furthermore, certain climatic conditions are crucial for the survival of *Xenopsylla cheopis*, the rat flea. According to studies done by the Plague Research Commission in India in 1908, the optimal conditions for the hatching of flea larvae are temperatures of between 18.3°C and 29.4°C and humidity of 70%; the flea cannot survive when humidity falls below 70%. The optimal temperature for the spread of disease is determined by the climatic conditions pertaining six weeks before the outbreak, and not by the weather at the time of the outbreak. Ideal conditions for an epidemic, according to the Commission, were temperatures of between 10°C and 29.4°C (or between 50°F and 85°F); temperatures above or below these figures caused a diminution of the disease, as happened during outbreaks in Bombay and Hong Kong at the beginning of the twentieth century. Moreover, observers of plague outbreaks in Hong Kong and India in 1894-1895 noted unusual weather conditions – higher than normal temperatures and unusually high rainfall – preceding or accompanying outbreaks of plague.[37]

However, the early years of the fourteenth century are presented in the contemporary records as years of exceptional rain and unusual cold. Curt Weikinn has catalogued all the references to weather during the Middle Ages and concluded that references to bad weather are much more frequent in the last two centuries of the Middle Ages. A study of the weather in Ireland by Dr M. Lyons indicates that increasing rainfall in particular during this period wrought havoc with harvests and resulted in food shortages, famine and disease.[38] In 1315-1318 wet winters were followed by rainy summers, resulting in failed harvests and widespread famine. *The Annals of Connacht* describe the period as one that brought 'many afflictions in all parts of Ireland: very many deaths, famine and many strange diseases, murders, and intolerable storms as well'. Bad weather continued for the next three years. In November 1316 a big storm damaged the belfry of Christ Church Cathedral along with other buildings in Dublin, and in 1318, according to the annals, Dublin saw 'snow the like of which had not been seen for many a long year'. Great winds are reported in 1324 and from 1329-1330 come reports of floods on the Boyne, storms and incessant rain in Dublin leading to shortages, high prices and even famine in the Dublin area. There were outbreaks of smallpox and influenza in the 1320s, and crop failure in 1321 and 1328. Nor did the weather in the 1330s and 1340s follow its usual patterns. In the winter of 1338-1339, for example, it is recorded that:

In the parts of Ireland the frost was so vehement, that Aven-Liffie, the river of Dublin, was so frozen that very many danced and leaped upon the ice of the said river, they played at football, and ran courses there: yea, and they made fires of wood and of turfe upon the same ice, and broyled herrings thereupon. This ice lasted very many dayes. And as for the snow also in the parts of Ireland, that accompanied the same frost, a man need not speake any more, seeing it was knowne to lye on such a wonderfull depth. This hard time of weather continued from the second day of December unto the tenth day of February: the like season was never heard of before, especially in Ireland.

Unusually wet winters and autumns are reported again in 1345, 1348 and 1349.[39]

Some scientific experts, such as J.F. Shrewsbury and G. Twigg, have argued that the climate in most of England, and by extension Ireland, would have been too cold to permit the spread of plague and that the mini Ice Age, which began about 1300, led to lower average temperatures, totally opposite to the conditions necessary for plague outbreaks. However, some recent studies on climate point to the likelihood that a warming trend developed in Europe during the plague years. While the 1330s and 1340s were a time of generally colder and wetter weather, there is some evidence that during 1348-1350 the warming winds of El Niño in Europe could have created higher than normal temperatures and more than normal rainfall even during the winter months. This would have created the optimal conditions for the rapid transmission of the *Y. pestis* bacillus. Moreover, the possibility that the Black Death was caused by a bacillus even more virulent than *Y. pestis* means that factors such as climate and ecological changes cannot be dismissed.

The theory that climate has a bearing on the outbreak and virulence of plague adds new significance to the comments of so many contemporary chroniclers, from Friar John Clyn, in Ireland to Gilbert li Muisis in Flanders and the Paris Medical Faculty, who all explicitly noted the temperate, wet weather during the years of the plague. Gilbert li Muisis writing from Flanders, commented on the oddness of the winter when, as he put it, '…there was not so much ice as would support the weight of a goose' but yet so much rain that rivers burst their banks and 'meadows became seas'. He added that the mildness of the winter and the heavy rains led many to fear the outbreak of illness in the month of March and in the summer months. The Paris Medical Faculty, in its report on the plague in October 1348, also commented on the unseasonable weather: a mild winter, a windy and wet spring, a changeable summer and, throughout all the seasons, excessive rain leading to pestilential air, which it considered the cause of the plague.[40] Wet winters and autumns are also recorded in southern England in 1345, 1348 and 1349. Ireland's weather would not have differed significantly from that of southern England or Flanders, and would likely have been even wetter and warmer. Clyn notes that 'this year was … fertile and abundant, although sickly and productive of great mortality'. Climatic studies thus support the observations of medieval chroniclers that unusual weather patterns accompanied plague outbreaks and, as we now know, provided favourable conditions for the diffusion of the epidemic.

THE 1340S: ON THE EVE OF THE BLACK DEATH

What was life like for the citizens of Dublin in the decade leading up to the Black Death? Contemporary records impart a sense of a city under siege, both militarily and economically. As in the rest of Ireland, the growth both economic and demographic that had characterised the earlier thirteenth century had come to an end by the beginning of the fourteenth century, thanks to famine, food shortages, political unrest and natural calamity. The silting up of the River Liffey presented ongoing problems to the commercial life of the city. Dublin had never been a wealthy city, and from an early stage its citizens had continuously complained of their impoverishment, particularly from taxes. As early as 1220 citizens were complaining to the King about the exactions of the Justiciar and his bailiffs, and that 'the city has thereby become so impoverished and odious to traders that none will come thither with merchandise'. In 1305, the city's arrears of rent were such that the mayor and bailiffs were ordered to seize the contents of ships and close the taverns until the arrears had been paid. People, and especially the poor, lived not only in a disease-prone environment, but also one in which hazards of all kinds were a continual threat, particularly fire. In 1283 a large part of the city of Dublin and the Holy Trinity Church were burnt and another fire in June 1304, according to contemporary sources, devastated the 'greater part' of the city.[41]

From the second decade of the century particularly, a host of factors left the city even more vulnerable and exposed: the Bruce Invasion of 1315-1318, Edward III's campaigns for which extra taxes were levied, the increasing threat from the Gaelic-Irish in Leinster, as well as the growing weakness of Leinster generally. Villages to the south of the city were frequently raided by the Gaelic-Irish of Wicklow, leaving the city itself even more vulnerable. For example, a notice from 1326 reported that:

> there are no buildings in Senekyl; once there were, but they are now burned and thrown down by the Irish felons. Nine score five acres of the same demesnes which used to be under the lord's ploughs, waste and untilled for the want of tenants because near the Irish malefactors.[42]

Dublin then suffered severely during the Bruce Invasion when the Scottish forces came as far as Castleknock. Because the city's walls were so weak, the panic-stricken citizens burned the suburbs in order to impede Bruce's progress towards the city. The strategy was successful in diverting the Bruces, but the fire spread into the city itself, destroying much of it. This had a long-standing and direct effect on the revenues of the government and of the city, and forced the City Council to make numerous requests for royal aid in the ensuing years and for remission of the city's fee farm – the fixed annual payment owed by cities to the King. In 1316, the city's farm was remitted. Again, in 1319, the mayor and Commonalty of Dublin requested exemption from the farm for a number of years because of the burning of the suburbs, a request repeated in 1334. And in the same year the Prior of the Hospital of St John the Baptist outside the New Gate of Dublin complained of the Hospital's impoverishment due to the attacks of the Scots and Irish and the burning of the suburbs of the city. The many protests of the Great Council to the King about the poverty of the English lieges in general would also have included the citizens of Dublin who were foremost in that group.[43]

Added to their economic woes was the increasing lawlessness affecting towns in the mid-fourteenth century as the effectiveness of the central administration waned. The Gaelic-Irish in Leinster inhabited the poorer land above 600 feet and, contemporary annals would suggest, suffered particularly from the famines and bad weather afflicting the country at the end of the thirteenth century. Not surprisingly then, their raids on the richer settlements of the Anglo-Irish became more frequent from the latter decades of the thirteenth century, particularly on the royal manors south of Dublin, and became particularly fierce in times of scarcity, famine and pestilence. In 1316, the common folk of Dublin were complaining about the 'general war of the Irish who daily menace the city', that the Irish enemies seized them and their goods whenever they ventured out of the city, and they warned that this together with the impending invasion of the Scots, would ruin the city. Hugh Lawless, a tenant on the royal demesne at Bray, complained that his lands lay totally waste and uncultivated because the Irish had invaded and burned them and because they had been devastated by the Scots. In Dalkey, in 1326, burgage rents could not be levied because of the war with the Irish. Even in the royal demesnes in Newcastle Lyons, tenants were so impoverished by war that they claimed they could no longer pay their rent.[44] Though travel had resumed between the city and towns to the south, such as Carlow and Kilkenny, as is suggested by the new bridges that were built across the Liffey and Barrow in 1319-1320, this did not last long. The difficulties of travelling to Dublin became such that in 1345 a royal decree requested that the exchequer and common bench be removed from Dublin 'to a safe place' for security reasons. Even trade between towns was hampered and, in 1340, the Justiciar ordered the arrest of evil doers who waylaid merchants, saying that because of their activities the merchants did not dare to travel. Settlers fled some outlying areas completely, moving within the city's walls for protection, and in time fled the country altogether for England, leaving some areas decaying and tenantless. Numerous areas and castles surrounding Dublin were deserted because of poverty and destruction by the Irish. The problem of absenteeism then became one of the most pressing problems in the decades leading up to the plague. This affected Dublin particularly, because of the strength of the MicMhurchadha in Wicklow who took advantage of the Black Death in Dublin and surrounding villages to wage their own attacks on the colony.[45]

In such straitened circumstances, blame was placed on various quarters, the most reviled being the royal administrators in Ireland. These were the 'new English', or 'English by birth', that is men who in recent decades were no longer the Anglo-Irish magnates – the 'English by blood' – of hitherto, but 'new' English officials sent to staff the King's government in Dublin and to root out the corruption prevalent among the Anglo-Irish officials. Their increasing efficiency, and above all their efficiency in exacting taxes, became the object of citizens' ire. When, in 1341, Anglo-Irish nobles and their supporters held a convention at Kilkenny in opposition to the Justiciar, the annalist of St Mary's Abbey, Dublin tells us that 'the land of Ireland was at the point to have been lost for ever out of the King of England's hand'. He writes of divisions between those who were 'English by birth and English in blood' and complains of the personal wealth accumulated by the King's ministers in Ireland at the expense of the King himself. Feelings against the Justiciar, Ralph d'Ufford, ran so deep, the St Mary's annalist tells us, that on his death in Dublin on 9 April 1346,

> The clergy and people both of the land, for joy of his departure out of this life, with merry hearts doe leap, and celebrate a solemn feast of Easter. At whose death the floods ceased, and the distemperature of the aire had an end and in one word, the common sort truly and heartily praise the onley Son of God… [46]

Surviving records then depict Dublin in 1348 as a city under siege, its citizens concerned about taxes, the growing power of English-born officials, the rebellious activities in the south

of Maurice fitz Thomas, Earl of Desmond, the activities of
the MicMhurchadha in Leinster, the security and defences of
the city, food shortages and the weather. There were other
troubles too. Ecclesiastical circles were exercised by the
Archbishop of Dublin, Alexander de Bicknor, and his alleged
protection of heretics who had flocked into the city.[47] There
were some tentative indications of improvement in conditions in Dublin. Taxes were being collected throughout the
province of Leinster and in July 1349 Thomas de Rokeby was
appointed Justiciar, a man who was to prove himself popular
with the colonists. 'It might,' writes Dr Otway-Ruthven, 'have
seemed that the position had been stab-ilized and that further
recovery would be possible'.[48] In cities in England, the 1330s
and 1340s had seen an equilibrium and the beginnings of a
recovery from the recession of the earlier part of the century.
Had such signs of recovery in Dublin continued, perhaps the
city's history would have taken a different course. But the
advent of a *deus ex machina* – the plague with its devastating
effects on cities – ensured that any recent gains, whether real
or superficial, would be quickly lost. Depressed by war, economic hardship and frequent famine, the inhabitants of
medieval Dublin were not in any position to withstand the
rigours of a plague epidemic.

CHAPTER TWO

The Plague's Progress

EARLIER PLAGUES

Various plagues were reported in Ireland and in Dublin in earlier times. The first known reference to 'plague' is in the *Annals of the Four Masters* for the year 940 BC:

> Nine thousand of Parthalon's people died in one week, on Sean-Mhagh-Ealta-Edair, namely five thousand men and four thousand women.

Reputedly, the place became known as Taimhlacht Parthalóin and has been identified as the modern Tallaght, a suburb of Dublin. The name is based on the Irish word *támh* meaning pestilence or plague and *támhlacht* (or *taimhleacht*) meaning a communal burial ground for plague victims. The word has also entered into other place names in Ireland, suggesting that these places were used as burial grounds during times of pestilence.[1]

Whether these were outbreaks of bubonic plague is a disputed point since 'plague' or in Irish *pláigh* was a non-specific term. Bubonic plague is an ancient disease, having originated in Asia and the Middle East, one of the first areas to develop a population sufficiently dense to sustain epidemics. From there it spread to other parts of Asia and thence to Europe. Strains of *Y. pestis* have existed from at least prior to Justinian's Plague in 540, which was probably of the bubonic variety, though claims have been made for other pathogens, including Ebola. This plague led to a pandemic that lasted approximately 200 years, with outbreaks every ten to twelve years. Plague returned to Europe in a second pandemic in 1347, which some contend was a resurgence of Justinian's Plague, and remained endemic until after 1650, with outbreaks approximately every eleven years. In *A History of Bubonic Plague in the British Isles*, the bacteriologist and historian, J.F. Shrewsbury, argues that no pestilence in the British Isles before the fourteenth century can be identified as bubonic plague, since there is no evidence that the black rat had colonized Ireland or England at this stage. He suggests that most of the earlier epidemics were of confluent smallpox whose symptoms are similar to those of bubonic plague. Not all agree, however.[2]

The wave of pestilence that swept the country in the seventh century has been linked to Justinian's Plague, but this identification is doubtful. Moreover, the Irish annalists often specify the diseases they report. *The Annals of the Four Masters* in AD 543 recorded a plague called *blefed*, possibly smallpox, 'which swept away the noblest part of the human race'. In AD 664 an epidemic of *Buidhe Chonaill* is recorded, probably some form of yellow fever or possibly malaria. According to *The Annals of the Four Masters*, many people, ecclesiastic and lay, died during this plague. The Venerable Bede also described a great plague in England in AD 664 that killed 'a vast number of people' and then did 'equal destruction' in Ireland. In AD 675, the *Annals of Clonmacnoise* recorded 'a great leprosy' called the 'Poxe', or in Irish, *bolgach*. Over the next hundred years various outbreaks of the yellow plague, smallpox and other diseases continue to be reported.[3]

Subsequent 'plagues' were not likely to have been bubonic plague. In 1225 the *Annals of Loch Cé* recorded a *galar mór*, or a great fever, 'by which the towns used to be emptied, without a living man being left in them'. Famine and pestilence are mentioned frequently in tandem: for example the *Annals of Innisfallen*, Clyn's *Annals* and the *Annals of St Mary's Abbey, Dublin* for 1271 record a 'a great famine and grave pestilence in Ireland'. Another pestilence and famine is recorded in 1294 when the *Annals of St Mary's Abbey* note 'great scarcity and pestilence throughout Ireland in this year and the two years following', an observation echoed by Clyn, who adds that 'many people perished of the hunger'. Then in 1305 a Kilkenny chronicle records that 'a sickness called "pokkis" swept through the land' and in 1332, a disease called 'Mauses' ravaged the population, affecting both the elderly as well as the young.[4] The precise nature of these 'plagues' is not always clear. Pneumonia, pleurisy, smallpox and typhus fever, among other diseases were common. However, these were not the same as the 'great plague' or *pláigh mór* that arrived in 1348.

Whatever modern scientists may decide regarding the precise cause of this 'plague', it was clearly qualitatively different to all that had gone before.

THE PLAGUE'S ARRIVAL

Given people's familiarity with illness and disease in the medieval city, the Black Death cannot have been recognised for what it was in its initial stages, since its early symptoms of chills, fever and headache are non-specific. Even Europe's most prominent medical authorities at the time, such as Guy de Chauliac, the Pope's physician, did not immediately grasp its seriousness. However, its aetiology and mortality were such that its unprecedented quality was soon recognised. This is reflected in the names attributed to it in the languages of Europe: *mortalitas prima, maximae mortalitates, magna mortalis, das Grosse Sterben, la Mortalega Grande, de Grote Sterfte, An Pláigh Mór,* The Great Dying …everywhere, its 'unheard-of mortality' was noted and reported. Not surprisingly then, surviving accounts of the plague are couched in apocalyptic imagery, since plague was traditionally seen as one of the Four Horsemen of the Apocalypse.

Plague mortality in medieval cities was high, not only because of their population density, nor because of the inhabitants' poor immunological health, but because they were centres of trade and therefore open to the movement of goods and people by which the plague traversed Europe and Asia. Moreover, the huge stores of grain stored in many ports provided ideal conditions for the propagation of the plague bacterium and its vector. The story of the plague's rapid transmission to Western Europe is well known. The outbreak of 1347–1349 would seem to have originated in the steppes of Central Asia and Mongolia where *Y. pestis* is endemic. Epidemics usually follow commercial trade routes, and the Black Death was no exception. With the opening up of trade routes in the East the bacillus was brought westward, carried by infected rats, which travelled in ships or migrated overland towards Central Asia, or by fleas carried in the merchandise of Mongol nomads from Eastern into Central Asia in the late 1320s. The disease then spread from Central Asia to the Black Sea and Southern Russia in 1345–1346. From there it travelled, overland or by sea, to the Crimea and thence, at least according to some sources, in Genoese trading vessels from the port of Caffa to Italy and Egypt in 1347, though it undoubtedly followed a number of other routes also. It then spread rapidly throughout Europe, jumping from port to port in the spring and summer of 1348.[5] Contemporary chroniclers repeatedly emphasise the speed of its transmission. The account by Henry Knighton, for example, captures some of its relentless progress through England:

> Then a lamentable plague travelled by sea to Southampton and on to Bristol, where almost the whole population of the town perished, snatched away, as it were, by sudden death, for there were few who kept their beds for more than two or three days, or even half a day. And thence cruel death spread everywhere with the passage of the sun.[6]

From either England or mainland Europe, the plague was brought to Ireland. Summer was undoubtedly the period of briskest trade and travelling, when weather and maritime conditions would have been most favourable to shipping; this is also the period when the bubonic form of plague is at its most virulent. Consequently, given a raging epidemic on the Continent and in England, it was inevitable that the epidemic would have been conveyed to Ireland in the strongholds of trading vessels or in the goods of merchants, or directly by human carriers of the pathogen. According to contemporary sources, it reached Dublin and Drogheda in July or early August 1348, carried perhaps by ships travelling between Bristol and Dublin. However, it had reached Bristol at the earliest on 24 June and at the latest on 1 August; the close timing between its arrival in Bristol and in Dublin and Drogheda suggests that the plague could have been brought directly from the Continent. However, since this disease does not depend solely on the prior infection of rats and could equally have been transmitted directly from person to person, one may not discount the possibility that the disease was brought directly by infected persons travelling from Bristol or Chester.

Contemporary witnesses do not wholly agree on the exact points of entry. According to Friar Clyn, the plague started at Howth or Dalkey outside Dublin and at Drogheda, but the Nenagh annalist notes it as beginning in Drogheda and then spreading to Dublin and the surrounding countryside.[7] That it made its first appearance in either Dalkey or Howth is not surprising given that Dalkey had for many years been used as the deep-sea anchorage for the port of Dublin, which was too shallow. Goods were unloaded at Dalkey and then shipped in lighter vessels into Dublin. In the holds of these ships were the rats and fleas that would bring bubonic plague within the walls of the city. Once in port, the black rat abandons the ships and burrows in the port areas. Or, if the infected fleas are man-carried, the fleas quickly move into the local colonies of rats, their natural hosts, and transmit the bacillus to the rats. This process may take only two weeks or less. Clearly the process of transmission would have been even more rapid in the event of an infectious disease.

News of its dissemination travelled almost faster than the plague itself, and contemporary sources clearly indicate that some at least were aware that this disease had already been spreading elsewhere and were fully aware of its lethal and unprecedented quality. The annalist of St Mary's Abbey, Dublin, for example, writes of the first and greatest pestilence (*prima pestilentia et maxima*) in Ireland which had begun earlier in other lands. According to Friar Clyn, the plague raged in Dublin between August and Christmas, causing 'unheard-of' mortality:

> There was hardly a house in which one only had died but as a rule man and wife with their children and all the family went the common way of death.

It is quite likely however that the plague broke out even earlier than Friar Clyn attests, as it would take a while for the disease to become rooted and be disseminated, and its earliest victims may not have been recognised as such. Equally likely is that its death toll continued even beyond the date of 25 December. Studies elsewhere have shown that an outbreak of plague lasted on average from nine to twelve months, though its most severe effects tended to be concentrated in a period of about three months. Outbreaks of the plague in London in the early seventeenth century

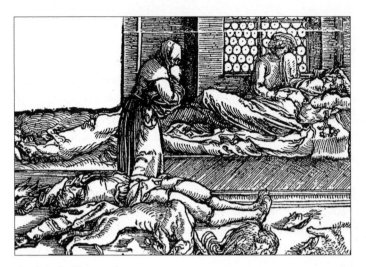

Death in the Homestead.

coincided with the summer and autumn months, with the highest mortality recorded between the end of July and the end of September. In Levett's studies of the Black Death in the estates of the diocese of Winchester, incidents began to appear in April-May 1348, but no significant mortality was felt until April-June 1349, and by October-November 1349 mortality had levelled off. Plague broke out in London in Autumn 1348 and raged there through winter and spring, and seems to have been most virulent between February and Easter. A similar pattern probably characterised the plague's progress in Dublin, but Clyn had by then turned his attention to his own city of Kilkenny, which had also fallen prey to the epidemic. Very soon after he died himself, and no other chronicler took up his account of the plague's progress.[8]

MORTALITY

One of the reasons why plague became such a feared disease was not the pain or the illness it caused, but the fact that its mortality rate was so high, higher even than that of smallpox or cholera. The plague of 1348 would seem to have been far more virulent than later outbreaks in the fourteenth and fifteenth centuries and certainly far more virulent than modern outbreaks of *Y. pestis*. The recognition of this has led recent historians to posit higher figures for plague dead than has been the case among historians in the past. In England, for example, most estimates now propose a death rate of between 40% and 55% (or more in certain areas) during the 1347-1349 outbreak.

Of crucial significance in considering the issue of mortality is the nature of the bacillus itself. The three-fold character of plague is well known: septicaemic, pneumonic and bubonic in decreasing order of severity, though these divisions are not watertight as plague has a protean character. Most experts claim that the bubonic and pneumonic strains raged together in Europe in 1348, at least in the opening stages. Bubonic plague is a contagion, most often transmitted by the bite of an infected flea, and rarely spreads directly between humans. Pneumonic plague is an infection of the lungs caused by the direct transmission of bacilli from an infected human to another, primarily by air-borne droplets, though contamination can also occur by inhaling the faeces of an infected flea. It would seem to occur only in cold weather. Since pneumonic plague cannot survive long on its own, the bubonic form dominates, but there is weighty epidemiological evidence that when plague invades virgin territory, it is apt to appear in its pneumonic form, at least in the first two or three months. The less common septicaemic form is transmitted by a flea bite directly into the bloodstream, causing the skin to turn purple. This form can also be transmitted very effectively by the human flea, *Pulex irritans*.[9]

These three strains of plague differ significantly. Bubonic plague affects the lymphatic system first and though the initial symptoms are non-specific, it becomes recognizable by painful swellings or buboes in the groin, armpits or upper neck, chills, a prickling sensation and giddiness, a staggering gait and eventually hallucinations and delirium. Death occurs within a week for an average of 60% of those infected, though the span can veer between 50% and 90%. Bubonic plague can range from mild cases to the most severe and the incidence is higher if infection occurs in the early stages of the outbreak. Since pneumonic plague attacks the lungs initially, its symptoms are expectoration, especially the spitting up of blood; death occurs within one to three days and case mortality is approximately 96%. The septicaemic type attacks very rapidly, and victims in modern outbreaks of the disease have died within a few hours without displaying any of the symptoms normally associated with plague, such as buboes. Mortality is 100%.

There are also significant variations in the transmission patterns of each form. In general the distribution of bubonic plague in the human population is slow as it depends on the prior infection of fleas by rats and this in turn is affected by the density of the rat and flea populations. Climate is a significant factor. Cold weather slows its rate of transmission since the black rat needs warmth, the rat flea needs temperatures between 15°C and 20°C and the bacillus thrives in temperatures of about 25°C. Furthermore, the flea needs relatively high humidity to propagate. Therefore, spring and early summer or late summer-early autumn were the times when bubonic plague was at its most severe in Europe. However, plague can also be transmitted by the human flea, which thrives in cold weather. Further, pneumonic plague and the very rare septicaemic form are dependent not on rat and flea density, but on certain environmental and climatic conditions and on a high degree of infection among humans. These strains are far more virulent and rapid, have a much higher infection rate and thrive in colder, damper climates. Accordingly, the accounts of many contemporary chroniclers emphasizing the suddenness of some deaths and the wet weather are substantiated by what we have come to know about the epidemiology of plague and its variant forms.

Some recent studies also suggest there may also be a connection between the levels of immunity, the socioeconomic conditions in a population and the form of plague that develops in that population. In 'The palaeopathology of urban infections', Dr K. Manchester writes:

> Individuals of low innate and acquired immunity upon contraction developed septicaemic plague and were rapidly eliminated from the infective scene. Because the innate immunity is loosely related to general health status, which itself is loosely related to social and economic conditions, septicaemic plague is more likely in the lowly classes of earlier society. Because acquired adaptive immunity in a population is dependent upon prior exposure to a pathogen, septicaemic plague is likely to be the earliest human expression, in historical terms, of plague. In general terms it is a truism that the initial clini-

cal manifestation of new infection in a virgin population is severe, but with a continued presence of the pathogen in the population there is attenuation of the disease. Pneumonic plague, as a systemic but less severe form, is likely to be a form of higher immunity, representing the expression in a higher socio-economic group. Bubonic plague, as a more localized bodily infection, is likely to be at the highest immunity status, being found in individuals of a higher socio-economic group, and of a later evolutionary stage in the development of plague in peoples.[10]

If this hypothesis is correct, then mortality among the poorer classes of Dublin in 1348 would have been significantly higher than among the wealthier. If, on the other hand, the Black Death appeared initially in its bubonic form, it is quite likely, given both modern scientific theory as well as contemporary fourteenth-century records, that it segued into the pneumonic form at a later stage. Some even argue that the bubonic and pneumonic strains raged simultaneously in Europe, a theory hotly disputed by others.[11] However, in the initial months, and certainly in the autumn months of 1348, it is quite likely that the pathogen assumed a pneumonic, possibly even septicaemic form. We know from other sources that 1348 was particularly wet and cool, therefore presenting the conditions conducive to pneumonia and pneumonic plague. Epidemiological evidence also indicates that plague, in invading virgin territory, may assume not only a pneumonic but also a septicaemic form. If that was the case in 1348, the plague could have been as virulent as contemporary chroniclers stressed, especially in the first months of the outbreak. So, the high mortality Friar Clyn recorded in Dublin would not have been impossible. Moreover, his graphic description of plague deaths in Ireland incorporates the symptoms of both bubonic and pneumonic strains: he describes the eruptions on the groin or under the armpit characteristic of, though not peculiar to, bubonic plague, but also the headaches and spitting of blood that distinguish pneumonic plague:

> Many died from carbuncles and boils and buboes which grew on the legs and under the arms, others from passion of the head, as if thrown into a frenzy; others by vomiting blood.

Clyn also emphasises the highly infectious nature of the pestilence:

> …the pestilence was so contagious that whosoever touched the sick or the dead was immediately infected and died, so that penitent and confessor were carried together to the grave.

As understood by Clyn and his contemporaries, contagion did not quite carry the same meaning that it does today. Rather it was understood to mean the corrupt air that is spread from person to person by exhalation, by touch, or even by look. Clyn's testimony again highlights the virulence of the Black Death that has troubled so many modern researchers. It also lends support to the theory that this was an outbreak of pneumonic plague, which is transmitted by direct contact between humans. In the early, more virulent phase of the plague's outbreak, while it raged throughout Dublin, the pneumonic form most likely dominated. As it moved beyond these first stages out to the surrounding countryside, it is not likely that it persisted in its pneumonic form, especially once it moved away from the areas of densest settlement.

Most annalists and historians emphasise the severe effects of the Black Death on towns and cities. In the densely settled, walled enclosures of the medieval town the plague spread quickly. 'That pestilence', wrote Friar Clyn, 'deprived of human inhabitants, villages and cities and castles and towns, so that there was scarcely found a man to dwell therein'. In England, Thomas Burton in his chronicle of Meaux Abbey wrote, 'the pestilence grew so strong that men and women dropped dead while walking in the streets, and in innumerable households and many villages not one person was left alive'. Knighton wrote of the city of Bristol being virtually wiped out. Similarly, a range of contemporary and near contemporary chroniclers further emphasize the severe effects of the plague on Ireland's coastal towns. Ralph Higden, the contemporary English chronicler, and the seventeenth-century historian, Barnes, both stressed its effects on the coastal towns of the Irish colony; Richard FitzRalph, the contemporary Archbishop of Armagh, noted the high mortality among maritime dwellers in Ireland and especially among fishermen and sailors. This echoed patterns elsewhere also, and the explanation offered at the time was that when corrupt air condensed, it lodged in low-lying areas, thereby creating the conditions for pestilence.[12]

The whole region around Dublin – the counties of Dublin, Meath, Louth and Kildare – was also severely affected by the plague. The explanations for this are various. Many of the villages were close to or on rivers, and on land below 600 feet, making them particularly open to the inroads of rats and

Death and the Merchant by Hans Holbein.

plague. Or the reason may lie in the trading activities of the region that allowed for direct transmission of the disease. By contrast, the hilly areas of County Wicklow, which were mostly in the hands of the Gaelic-Irish, seem to have escaped the plague. This had an important bearing on the security of Dublin and on the increasingly embattled position of its citizens.

Mortality among the Clergy, Public Officials and the Poor

Plague is no respecter of persons, and no particular group was spared, though it has been observed to strike certain groups in one outbreak and other groups in the next. This happened, for example, in San Francisco in 1900 when the Chinese community was largely affected, whereas in the subsequent outbreak of 1907 the Caucasian population, which had been spared in the first outbreak, was the locus of the disease. In Ireland, the plague of 1348 is reported to have hardly affected Gaelic-Irish areas but to have had severe effects later. Similarly, the nobility seems to have been spared during the outbreak of 1348, but was not during the outbreak of 1361. The outbreaks of 1361 and 1370 also particularly affected young people.

Mortality in 1348 was reputedly highest among the clergy throughout Europe, though clearly this must to some extent be a reflection of the fact that ecclesiastical records are more plentiful than those for other classes. The effects of the Black Death on European and English monasteries have been amply recorded, though those for Dublin are somewhat sketchy. There is no break in the succession of abbots in St Mary's Abbey, Dublin, nor of priors in the Priory of St John the Baptist. However, this does not necessarily signify that the plague did not affect these institutions, particularly given its devastation of the Franciscan house in Dublin.[13] Friar Clyn writes of the devastation wrought by the plague where, 'scarcely one alone ever died in a house but …all went the way of the Lord'. The only details he gives, however, are for the mendicant orders, and above all for his own order, the Franciscans. He records that by Christmas 1348, twenty-five Franciscans had died in Drogheda and twenty-three in Dublin; these numbers would

Death and the Abbot, Death and the Friar and *Death and the Bishop* by Hans Holbein. Holbein's woodcuts from 1538 popularised the images of the Dance of Death, which were among the most popular images of late medieval art and literature. According to one theory, the image originated in the practice, common during the Black Death, of men and women dancing to the music of drums and bagpipes as a way of warding off pestilence. In the artistic representation of the image, Death is presented as the Great Leveller, taking young and old, rich and poor alike.

have represented at least half of the total number of friars in these houses. How many more died we do not know as Friar Clyn himself died shortly after having recorded, on 6 March 1349, the deaths of eight Friars Preachers in Kilkenny.[14] Clyn's figures are quite credible, given that the popularity of the Franciscans, especially as confessors, would have exposed them to contagion. Moreover, since he also described symptoms indicative of the pneumonic form of plague, which has a high rate of infection and kills within two to three days, many more friars or inhabitants of these monasteries may have died than the records indicate.

Other religious houses were also affected. The Prior of Kilmainham, John Larcher, died in 1349, in circumstances that strongly suggest a plague death. In Spring 1349, he had become involved in a long-standing dispute between the archbishops of Dublin and Armagh. The Pope had asked Archbishop FitzRalph of Armagh to initiate an enquiry into the conduct of Alexander de Bicknor, Archbishop of Dublin, concerning his alleged protection of heretics who were flocking into the city from the Diocese of Ossory. The affair also raised old tensions about the primacy of the See of Armagh over that of Dublin. FitzRalph went to Dublin, probably in April/May 1349, and promptly excommunicated the Prior of Kilmainham who had supported de Bicknor. Then the prior suddenly fell ill and begged FitzRalph's forgiveness, a turnabout whose suddenness has led commentators to surmise he had been stricken with plague and knew he was about to die. However, Larcher died before his request was met and the forgiveness was then granted posthumously. If the suppositions about Larcher's fate are correct, this would indicate that the plague was still present in Dublin almost one year after its initial appearance. His successor, John Fitzrichard, was appointed in 1349, but died within a few months; no other deaths in the priory have been recorded.[15]

In St Patrick's Cathedral, Dublin, the deanery experienced a heavy mortality: Roger de Moclowe (or de Monte Lowe), appointed in 1348, died before he got possession; his successor, Hugh Earit, appointed in the same year, also died before entering office; in February 1349 Matthew de Brissells (or Briselee) was provided but he too died before the end of the year. The chancellor, Hugh de Calce, died in 1349. Among the other offices in the Cathedral, the treasurer died in 1349 as did the archbishop, though there is an unbroken line of precentors and archdeacons. The Prior of Christ Church, Robert de Hereford, died in 1348, having been in office for only two years. Outside the city, there are records of an unusual number of appointments from 1349-1350. The prebends of Castleknock, Rathmichael, Stagonil and five unnamed prebends all fell vacant at this time; two of these vacancies were due to the promotion of the previous incumbent to the archbishopric, the remainder to death, though the cause of death is not mentioned. Finally, the office of Vicar-General of the diocese and city of Dublin fell vacant in 1349, for in December of that year, Stephen, Prior of Holy Trinity, was appointed to the benefice. The presence of the Black Death is perhaps sufficient explanation for this unprecedented mortality and disruption.[16]

Calculating the total mortality for the Diocese of Dublin is not possible, however. Perhaps inferences could be drawn on the basis of mortality in English dioceses, though global figures for clerical deaths are difficult to determine and not only in Ireland. There is little agreement among historians of the plague elsewhere as to whether the clergy in particular suffered more

than any other section of the population. Their pastoral duties
would have exposed them more than other classes to infection,
but the far superior housing conditions of the non-mendicant
orders would also have protected them against plague, at least
of the bubonic variety. J.F. Shrewsbury contended that the
numbers cited for plague deaths among the clergy were exaggerated and that many vacancies arose from resignation or
flight. Recent studies, however, indicate otherwise. Studies of
the episcopal registers of the dioceses of Bath and Wells, Exeter,
Lichfield, York and Lincoln among others, all indicate an average death rate of approximately 40% to 50% for 1348, with a
rate of 70% and more for some deaneries in the dioceses of
Exeter, Coventry, Hereford and others.[17] Gwynn, in his study,
'The Black Death in Ireland' compared the dioceses of
Dublin and Exeter, which offered similarities in their coastal
location, their size, and the fact that both were among the
first places visited by the plague in their respective countries. In the Diocese of Exeter the average number of inductions to livings in normal times was three per month and
in Autumn 1348 no significant changes were recorded.
Change came in January 1349 when thirty-one inductions
to benefices were noted. The number rose steadily in the
succeeding months: thirty-five in February, sixty in March,
forty-three in April, forty-eight in May, forty-six in June,
thirty-seven in July, seventeen in August and a gradual
return to the average of three by the end of 1350. Gwynn
inferred a somewhat similar mortality in the Diocese of
Dublin. Definite figures, however, are impossible; perhaps
all that may safely be said is that the 1348 outbreak and
subsequent outbreaks 'reduced the number of religious of
both races in Ireland considerably'.[18]

In general, the wealthy and powerful in Dublin were almost certainly less affected, perhaps because they fled, just as Dublin's wealthy would abandon the city during later outbreaks of plague, or because they were protected by their stone houses, healthier immune systems, or some other unknown factor. This was a common pattern throughout Europe and some contemporary commentators were at pains to explain this variation in the plague's effects. The Oxford astrologer, Geoffrey de Meaux, offered this intriguing explanation:

> It was and is known to all astrologers that at the time of this eclipse the three superior planets were in the sign of Aquarius, where the fixed stars are not of the first magnitude and, save for one which is in the south, far distant from us, are lesser stars which signify the common people, and therefore the effect of the illness which they brought touched those people more…

Not that the plague spared the rich and prominent everywhere, however. Gilbert li Muisis in Tournai, for example, writes that mortality was greatest among the wealthy, although less among those who drank wine or removed themselves from corrupted air and did not visit the sick. Exposure was crucial, adds li Muisis:

> Others, who visited or lived among the sick, either became seriously ill or died; and they died especially in the streets in the market area, and more people died in the outskirts and in narrow lanes than in broad streets and marketplaces.[19]

Death and the Nobleman by Hans Holbein.

However, plague has always been largely a disease of the poor, and at various times has been known as the 'beggars' disease', the 'poor plague' and *miseriae morbus*. 'This sickness befell people everywhere,' wrote John of Fordun in his *Scotichronicon*, 'but especially the middling and lower classes, rarely the great'. Geoffrey le Baker also noted that incalculable numbers of the 'common' people died of the plague.

Elsewhere, for example in the cities of Rimini, Orvieto and Narbonne, records indicate that the plague attacked principally the poor, whose living conditions favoured the propagation of rats and fleas and whose depressed immune systems possibly contributed to the spread of disease. Surviving records in Ireland give very little indication of the plague's possible effects on this class. In fact, if the Black Death's main victims were the poor, perhaps it is not surprising that there are so few contemporary accounts of the plague in general in Ireland, since most of the surviving records focus on the landowning, governing and ecclesiastical spheres. That the poor of Dublin were both numerous and vulnerable is suggested by the frequent references to their plight in contemporary poems such as Hymn by Friar Michael, 'A Song on the Times' and 'A Satire'. In 'Hymn', for example, the poor man is described as 'hungir-bitte', weeping many a 'sorful tere' and crying, 'Hunger me haveth ibund'. Crowded into the alleys of certain streets, living on the streets or in inferior housing, these were the people most affected by the outbreak of 1348. Boccaccio highlights the heavy toll among the lower and middle classes in Florence:

> As for the common people and a large proportion of the bourgeoisie, they presented a much more pathetic spectacle, for the majority of them were constrained, either by their poverty or the hope of survival, to remain in their houses. Being confined to their own parts of the city, they fell ill daily in their thousands, and since they had no one to assist them or attend to their needs, they inevitably perished almost without exception. Many dropped dead in the open streets, both by day and by night, whilst a great many others, though dying in

their own houses, drew their neighbours' attention to the fact more by the smell of their rotting corpses than by any other means. And what with these, and the others who were dying all over the city, bodies were here, there and everywhere.[20]

Death and the Town Notables by Hans Holbein.

Not surprisingly, disposing of large numbers of bodies was a challenge to the authorities in a medieval city. Dublin, as noted already, was short of space and the sudden requirements for burial grounds for large numbers of poor could hardly have been met. For such people then, mass pit graves or an unmarked grave was all they could hope for.

Mortality among public officials was also high in many instances on the European mainland, since their duties did not allow them to flee the towns and cities as so many wealthier citizens could. Evidence for mortality among government officials in Dublin is scarce and what evidence exists indicates some difficulties, though no major hiatus. The Black Death came at a time of general disruption in the administration and the extent to which it undoubtedly aggravated this situation is difficult to estimate. The unsettled state of the administration is evident in that thirty justiciars or chief governors were appointed between 1324 and 1379, with the average term of tenure being only a few months. With the appointment of Ralph d'Ufford as Justiciar in July 1344 some continuity had been established and the average term increased to approximately two and a half years. However, during the years when the Black Death raged in Dublin, there is an unprecedented alteration of justiciars; three in the period November 1347–December 1349.

As noted already John Larcher, who was also Prior of Kilmainham, was dismissed for his involvement in altercations between the archbishops of Dublin and Armagh and died later in 1349 very probably of plague. He was succeeded for a short time by Walter de Bermingham, who then left Ireland soon after and died in England in 1350. His successor as deputy justiciar, John de Carew, remained in office for only three months, and does not again appear on the administrative lists, unusual in medieval Ireland since the same men often held office many times.[21]

PERIOD	JUSTICIARS/CHIEF GOVERNOR
June 1346–November 1347	Walter de Bermingham (appointed May 1346)
November 1347–April 1348	John Larcher (Deputy Justiciar)
April 1348–October 1349	Walter de Bermingham
October 1349–December 1349	John de Carew (Deputy Justiciar)
December 1349–March 1352	Thomas de Rokeby (appointed July 1349)
March 1352–June 1352	Maurice Rochfort (Deputy Justiciar)

In the records concerning other administrative officers, there is clear evidence of disruption, though that for mortality is sketchy.[22] In the available lists of Chancellors and Keepers of the Seal, John Larcher again served as chancellor until March 1348, while he was also acting justiciar. There isn't any chancellor recorded from then until April 1349 when John Darcy was appointed keeper; he remained in office until January 1350 and then disappears from the lists, even though his successor, William of Bromley, reappears later as treasurer. The gap between March 1348 and April 1349, while the plague was prevalent in Dublin, is a clear indication of the disruption caused in the business of the chancery.

In the treasury some dislocation is also evident as there seems to have been an unusual alteration of officials at this period:

PERIOD	TREASURER	DEPUTY TREASURER
August 1321–Hilary 1343	Eight treasurers appointed	Seven deputy treasurers appointed
May 1343–September 1349	John of Burnham	Robert Power (Baron of the Exchequer in Trinity, 1349)
Hilary 1348		Nicholas Allen (appears as treasurer after 1350)
Trinity 1348–Michaelmas 1349		Robert of Embleton (Baron of Exchequer after 1350)
September 1349–January 1350	Robert of Embleton (arrested in February 1350 and sent to England)	
September 1350–June 1360	Eight treasurers appointed	Eight treasurers appointed

Neither John of Burnham, treasurer until September 1349, nor Robert Power, deputy treasurer, appear again on the administrative lists. These are the only such instances recorded for the treasury. On the other hand, the Barons of the Exchequer seem to have been spared, except again for Robert Power, Baron of the Exchequer in Trinity 1349, who does not reappear. Of the other administrative offices, only the Escheator and Chamberlain of the Exchequer, John of Carrow, finally disappeared from the administrative lists in August 1349. Though there are many possible reasons for the unusual disappearance of these men, death by plague is certainly a plausible cause.

Within the administration of the City of Dublin itself, evidence suggests that the city's administrative officials may not have completely escaped. There seems to have been considerable dislocation in the administration, as is evident from the list of mayors and bailiffs for Dublin during 1343-1352:

PERIOD	MAYORS	BAILIFFS
1339-40	Kenewrek Sherman	John Callan, Adam de Louestoc
1340-41	Kenewrek Sherman	William Walsh, John Crek
1341-43	John Le Seriaunt	John Crek, Walter de Castleknock
1343-44	John Le Seriaunt	William Walshe, John Taylor
1344-45	John Le Seriaunt	William Walshe, John Callan
1345-46	John Le Seriaunt	William Walshe, Thomas Dod
1346-47	John Le Seriaunt	Walter Lusk, Rogert Grauntcourt
1347-48	Geoffrey Crompe	Walter Lusk, William Walshe
1348-49	Kenewrek Sherman	John Callan, John Dent
1349-50	Geoffrey Crompe	Roger Grauntcourt, Walter Lusk
1349-50	John Seriaunt	John Dent, John Bek
1350-51	John Bathe	Robert Burnell, Richard Heygrewe
1351-52	Robert de Moenes	John Dent, Peter Morville

Since mayors and bailiffs were appointed yearly, it is difficult to see whether there was any exceptional mortality in 1348-1350. Three mayors were appointed in 1348-1350. The first, Kenewrek Sherman, died later in the Dominican Priory in Dublin in February 1351. His successor, Geoffrey Crompe, was mayor from 1349-1350 and then disappears from the list, but it is not likely, though not impossible, that the plague would still be claiming victims in Dublin as late as 1350. The bailiffs for the period 1348-1349, John Callan and John Dent, were again appointed in 1349, 1351 and 1352, though the bailiffs for the first period in 1349-1350, Roger Grauntcourt and Walter Lusk, do not appear again at any later time. As with government officials, the same men held civic offices on more than one occasion, and their disappearance from the lists in 1348-1350 would seem at the least unusual. Moreover, the fact that there are two entries for the year 1349-1350, the only instance of such between 1300 and 1447, points to at least a temporary dislocation of business during the plague years. There is no break however in the succession of sheriffs in County Dublin, Adam Talbot holding the office throughout the period 1336-1356.[23]

The disruption caused by the pestilence of 1348, as well as its subsequent outbreaks, affected not only the day-to-day running of the administration but added considerably to the perilous state of the colonial administration in general. It severely affected the city's defence problems because of its effects on areas surrounding the city and particularly on the manors that supplied the city's provisions and acted as buffers for the city against the attacks of the Gaelic-Irish of Wicklow. A number of scattered references hint at its toll. The royal manors of Newcastle Lyons, Tassagard, Crumlin, Oughterard and Castlewarny were severely affected by plague, as were the manors of the archbishop at Finglas, Swords, Clondalkin and Tallaght. The effects on the city and on the administration would continue to be felt for decades to come.[24]

TOTAL MORTALITY

What general conclusions can be drawn from the existing evidence, meagre though it is at times? Analogy with other European cities would suggest a high death toll. Huge num-

bers of people died in Europe's cities, though those cited by
the medieval chroniclers have to be treated with some cau-
tion, since there weren't any reliable instruments for counting
the dead. In Genoa half the population died, in Padua two
thirds, in Verona three quarters. In Florence, according to
Villani, three out of every five died and Boccaccio estimated
that 100,000 died in Venice and Florence. In Siena, in 1348,
there were eleven times more deaths than normal and mortality there was well over 50%. Petrarch estimated that 40,000
died in Parma and Reggio within six months. In San
Gimignano in Italy the number of deaths declined by more
than half after the plague; in Albi in the South of France the
number of deaths fell from 2,669 in 1343 to 1,200 in 1357.
Avignon was devastated, with Knighton reporting that 1,312
people died in one day alone, and in Paris, the chronicler of
St Denis reported 800 deaths in one day, 50,000 in Paris altogether and another 16,000 in St Denis. Two hundred people
were reported to have been buried in Smithfield Cemetery in
London between 2 February and 12 April 1349. In Norwich,
the Guildhall recorded that 57,374 people died. Modern estimates of the numbers of dead are not quite so high.
Hollingsworth, for example, estimated about 17,300 to have
died in London, and about 17,000 in Norwich.[25]

Richard FitzRalph of Armagh, who had no reason to dis-
simulate, calculated that the plague had destroyed more than
two thirds of the English nation in Ireland. Though this is not
a precisely calculated estimate and may be exaggerated, it still
points to a very high mortality among the colonists in Ireland,
many of whom lived in Dublin and in surrounding villages
and counties. Friar Clyn, who has a reputation of being a normally reliable chronicler, writes that 14,000 died in Dublin

De*ath and the Judge* by Hans Holbein.

between 8 August and 25 December. It is an unusual figure, lacking the roundness of the figures usually cited by medieval chroniclers, and we don't know how Clyn reached it. Creighton, in his *History of Epidemics in Britain*, dismissed Clyn's figures, and saw them 'merely as illustrating the inability of early writers to count correctly up to large numbers'. Yet, the precision of Clyn's dates and of his estimate gives pause. His figure of 14,000 in fact indicates an average daily mortality of 100, and perhaps Clyn calculated his overall figure on the basis of a daily reckoning, taken in the early months of the outbreak in Dublin. Such mortality is not impossible during the early, more virulent stages of an epidemic. The overall figure of 14,000 may be exaggerated, though by how much is an intriguing question.[26]

Clyn's estimates of Dublin's mortality were dismissed completely by J.F. Shrewsbury in *A History of Bubonic Plague in the British Isles* on the basis of findings from outbreaks of bubonic plague in India in 1898. Shrewsbury argued that since rat and flea density in India in 1898 would have been similar to that of late medieval Dublin, absolute mortality rates would therefore have been similar: namely, no higher than 25% of the population. On demographic grounds he also disputed the figure, claiming that 10,000 deaths of women should be added to Clyn's figure, which would result in a mortality rate requiring a population of about 96,000, clearly an impossible figure. However, Shrewsbury's arguments are not altogether convincing. There is no reason to suppose that Clyn, in referring to 'men', is speaking of the male species only: he uses the generic word *homo* meaning 'human being' and not *vir* or 'man' in distinction from 'woman'. Clyn may also have included the suburbs in his reckoning, and many experts speculate that most of Dublin's population lived outside its walls. In fact, according to Dr Howard Clarke, as many as 80% of Dubliners may have lived outside the city's walls in clusters of suburbs during the early fourteenth century. Further, most epidemiologists now agree that one cannot compare the mortality figures of plague in modern times with those for the Middle Ages, as the medieval plague would seem to have been far more virulent. As noted already, recent scientific studies of *Y. pestis* reinforce this view. Finally, Shrewsbury did not even allow for the possibility of pneumonic plague, and Clyn's own testimony clearly points to symptoms of pneumonic plague among Dublin's victims. In short, while the figure of 14,000 deaths in Dublin seems high, its plausibility is not denied by Shrewsbury's arguments.[27]

Because precise calculations of the city's pre-Black Death population are not possible, calculating the number who died remains problematic. If one accepts the more cautious figure of around 25,000 suggested by Hollingsworth for Dublin's population, then Clyn's figures are within the bounds of possibility and not out of line with mortality rates reported in European cities of similar size. Bearing in mind that plague is extremely virulent in its initial phases, a case mortality in the region of 40% to 50% is quite possible for Dublin. This figure is also in line with most recent estimates of overall plague mortality. While historians' estimates of overall plague mortality vary widely, from Shrewsbury's 5% to Ziegler's 33%, more recent calculations, especially for England, posit mortality rates of 30% to 45% in 1348. Some claim that a mortality rate as high as 40% to 60% was common in many areas and that the average mortality was probably around 47% to 48% during the first eighteen months of the plague.[28]

However, such estimates have to remain very tentative, given the wide variation in the plague's incidence throughout Europe. Mortality in densely populated, urbanised Flanders was in the region of 15% to 25%, but in rural Holland it exceeded 30%, in the rural Midi of France 45%, in sparsely populated Scandinavia 45% and in Iceland over 50%. Some figures put Europe's and England's population in 1430 at half what it had been at the end of the thirteenth century, and argue that the pre-plague population levels were not reached again until the 1600s. The demographer Livi-Bacci is somewhat more cautious: on the basis of studies in Italy, largely of its cities and towns, he suggests that between 1347 and the first half of the fifteenth century, Europe lost between 30% and 40% of its population, and regained its pre-plague population of 74 million in the 1550s. A rough consensus of historians' estimates of overall mortality in Europe would be a figure ranging from 35% to 45%, with a preference for rates at the higher end of the scale, especially in relation to urban mortality.

Such a mortality rate for the plague of 1348 and its successors may also be conservatively inferred for Dublin and some of the surrounding region. The only area outside the city for which we have any precise figures is the township of Colemanstown in the royal manor of Newcastle Lyons. According to a petition in 1392 from the tenants to the King, there were only three tenants remaining on the manor, the other sixteen having been 'cut off by the late pestilence'. If these figures are correct, then plague mortality in this township was in the region of 84%. Such a high mortality in one area from accumulated outbreaks of the plague is not unprecedented. But to what extent this instance can be taken as typical of the mortality in other regions surrounding Dublin is a debatable point. A mortality rate of 84% throughout County Dublin would surely have disrupted the administration more completely and would have left the economy far more shattered than the surviving evidence corroborates.[29]

The plague's overall effect on demographic decline in Dublin in the later Middle Ages was a cumulative one. Thanks to famines and warfare, the population of the city, as of the Anglo-Irish colony in general, had already been in decline for some decades before the Black Death broke out. However, many epidemiologists argue that exogenous factors such as pestilence are, in the end, ultimately responsible for large-scale demographic downturns. The effect of the plague, this new and recurring disease, was crucial in finalizing the downward demographic trend in Dublin, and helped to make Dublin an even more beleaguered city than it already was. In 1360, the Great Council of Ireland, in the context of an urgent petition to the King for help against the Irish enemy, complained that because the plague was 'so great and so hideous among the

English lieges and not among the Irish', it had worsened all the city's other long-standing problems.[30]

Dublin's population continued to decline, by as much as two thirds until the middle of the sixteenth century. Using guild membership figures, Dr Gearóid Mac Niocaill calculated its population would have been only about 6,000 in 1476, though he acknowledges this figure to be 'the merest guesswork'. Nor did the population recover quickly. By using data from tithes and various other sources to calculate the number of persons Dublin could support, Mac Niocaill estimated 8,000 inhabitants in the city in 1540. The fact that the population of Dublin was still so low in the mid-sixteenth century must reflect the effect of the crisis mortality engendered by the Black Death and its subsequent outbreaks in the fourteenth and fifteenth centuries. The continuing drain on the population had many consequences for a city already weakened by the outbreak of 1348. In many respects a study of the overall demographic effects of the plague of 1348-1350 cannot be considered apart from these later, related outbreaks. Had the outbreak of 1348 been the only one, the population of Dublin, though not robust in the years before the plague, would have recovered, as it would after the devastating plague of 1650. But whereas the outbreak of 1650 was the last major instance of plague in Ireland, this was not the case in 1348. Plague was to recur at regular intervals, with the result that sustained recovery was not possible and a chronic pattern of crisis mortality set in. The long-term demographic effects of this cannot be underestimated. While figures for Ireland are not available, again an analogy highlights the continuing effects of the plague. A study of the effect of the fifteen outbreaks of plague in Christ Church, Canterbury during the fifteenth century has shown that the disease accounted for 20% of all deaths. As Dr John Hatcher has written of post-plague England:

> ...it must be stressed that it is mistaken to assume that demographic decline could only be effected by national epidemics of spectacular proportions. On the contrary there is every reason to believe that the cumulative impact of lesser and local epidemics could be decisive, the more so if the young were afflicted in disproportionately high numbers.

Furthermore, as happened elsewhere in the later decades of the century, though not in the immediate wake of the plague, the number of marriages, conceptions and births probably declined, aggravating the population decline caused by plague mortality. [31]

Finally, the population in Dublin was not being replenished by immigration. Elsewhere in Europe and in England the urban population was continually supplemented by immigration from rural areas and, in fact, immigration constituted the principal means of population increase. This was not true of Dublin because of strictures against the immigration of the Gaelic-Irish. Though the Gaelic-Irish in Dublin became somewhat more numerous in the course of the fifteenth century, in general they were granted only secondary status and their entry was controlled. In fact, Dublin's population experienced not immigration but emigration that gathered force in the course of the century.

Population recovery became evident only from the beginning of the seventeenth century but it was slow: even as late as 1650, only 20,000 are estimated to have been living in Dublin. From that point on, population recovered rapidly and is estimated to have reached 130,000 in the 1750s. On the basis of these estimates, one could then conclude that the population of Dublin did not recover its pre-plague level until the mid-seventeenth century, about the same time that plague made its last major appearance in Europe. This too is the demographic pattern that characterized Europe in general between the fourteenth and the seventeenth centuries. According to Hollingsworth, among others, the number of people alive in 1444 was about the same as in 1086 and, not until the 1600s did the population rise to the level it had reached before the Black Death.[32]

Thanks in part to demographic changes, the plague helped to introduce some radical long-term changes into the economy of medieval cities in general. Its most devastating effects were felt in the cities of Italy where it brought about long-lasting institutional changes. The population of cities in Northern Germany declined, as did others in the Lowlands such as Ypres, Ghent and Bruges. In England, cities such as Winchester, Oxford and Lincoln lost their former prominence, while others such as Coventry developed. Dublin's population also declined in the course of the fifteenth century, with an accompanying contraction in its economic activity. The consequences of the plague clearly differed from one city to the next, and while similar patterns can be detected across the medieval Catholic, pre-industrial cities of Europe, nevertheless there are important differences between the experiences and the responses of each city.

CHAPTER THREE

Responses to the Plague

RELIGIOUS RESPONSES

Mortality figures, to borrow a remark made by Dr Kevin Whelan in writing about the nineteenth-century famine in Ireland, 'bankrupt the imagination as to the degree of human anguish contained in them'.[1] Mere numbers tell us very little about the human experience of the plague. As the people of Dublin witnessed the deaths in their midst and the seemingly inexorable march of the plague, what were their responses? What measures did they take to deal with it and minimise its impact?

Contemporary sources do not always help illuminate these questions. The reason is partly that the effects of the Black

Death were felt most among the poor and among the nameless citizens of the city and, unfortunately, the narratives of such people were not the stuff of Irish medieval chronicles and annals. Another reason may be that in the minds of contemporaries, and especially of those drawing up official documents, the plague was one catastrophe among many, hardly deserving of special mention. Moreover, with each new visitation, plague came to be seen as an almost seasonal occurrence and, except for a particularly lethal outbreak, was often hardly mentioned. This happened, for example, in Orvieto in Italy, a city where the plague's devastation was very extensively documented. In discussing the causes of the crisis that affected the city at the end of the century, the City Council accorded last place to the plague, which it saw as less immediately pressing than the incessant warfare in the surrounding region.[2]

In 1348, however, plague was everywhere: an unknown and terrifying reality. Fear and panic were the first and most immediate responses, and many would have shared the sense of horror captured by Friar John Clyn whose final words express the desolation of a man facing what must have seemed like the end of life as he knew it:

And I, Brother John Clyn of the Friars Minor in Kilkenny have written in this book the notable events which befell in my time, which I saw myself or have learned from men worthy of belief. So that notable deeds shall not perish with time, and be lost from the memory of future generations I, seeing these many ills, and the whole world lying, as it were, in the wicked one among the dead, waiting for death till it come, have committed to writing what I have truly heard and examined;

and lest the writing perish with the writer or the work with the workman, I leave parchment for continuing the work, if haply any man survive or any of the race of Adam escape this pestilence and continue the work which I have commenced.

These words suggest that Clyn was aware of his own impending death. He did not write any further in his chronicle and another hand closed his annals at this point with the terse *obit*: 'Here, it seems, the author died', surely of plague.

The sense of terror found a language in the traditional apocalyptic imagery of the Bible: the plague was part of the history of the human race as foretold in the *Book of Revelation*,

Knock, Devil, Knock: From the fourteenth to the seventeenth centuries, evil spirits were believed to be the bearers of plague. Here in this German print from 1508, the Devil prowls around a town, bringing death to selected households.

one of those biblical plagues that will signal the end of history. Friar Clyn gives to his description of the plague's ravages an apocalyptic frame that would not have seemed out of place or *de trop* to his contemporaries:

> There will be many battles and much slaughter, unrelenting famine and widespread mortality of men, revolutions in kingdoms; the land of the heathens will be converted …More people in the world have died in such a short time of plague, hunger or other infirmity than has been heard of since the beginning of time. An earthquake, which extended for miles, has overwhelmed, swallowed and destroyed cities, villages and castles.[3]

Such accounts are clearly an admixture of images from the *Book of Revelation*, hearsay and exaggeration, yet they were the common currency of the time. They capture the horror people felt and give expression to the ways in which they tried to make sense of the unprecedented mortality.

However, far from adopting radically different ways of behaving, people turned to traditional consolations and supports. As Dr Paul Binski in this regard writes,

> The impact of exogenous shocks to a culture or an economy is linked inexorably to endogenous response – cultures respond in certain ways to events because they are already predisposed to do so.

Once the initial panic subsided, more considered responses in general accorded with people's understanding of disease, its causes, its transmission and remedies. The primal cause of the plague was the wrath of God and the general recognition was that little could be done about that, except to try and avert or assuage it. Not surprisingly then, people turned to religion for support and consolation. Processions were held, special plague Masses said, litanies recited. The plague elicited genuine religious fervour. In England, for example, the number of ordinations to the priesthood rose in the years immediately following the plague, by contrast to the declining numbers before its outbreak. Of course, the motivation here may not have always been pristine pure and no doubt mercenary considerations were also at play here, now that the Church's ranks had been so severely depleted and more employment opportunities were on offer.[4]

In the sure expectation of sudden death, many rushed to confession and penance, since the belief that sin is the ultimate cause of death is deeply embedded in Christian thought. The Pope, according to the chronicler Knighton, sent letters '...asserting that all those misfortunes had come upon mankind because of their sins'. It was a view widely shared – 'these pestilences were purely for sin', as the poet Langland put it. In the event of a sudden death, people feared not so much hell as purgatory, so confession and absolution became highly prized. There was a significant increase in the number of requests to the Pope for the right of *confessionale* – that is, the right to choose one's own confessor with the power to grant full remission of sins at the hour of death, a power hitherto reserved to the Pope. These requests were clearly inspired by the fears and beliefs of lay people, not by any ecclesiastical requirements. The sharp rise in the number of requests at this time may not be explained solely by reference to the developing efficiency of the Curia in processing such requests,

Plague sick in front of the church.

nor to the practise of requiring a fee for indulgences, which became increasingly common during the Avignon Papacy. In Dublin we find not only clerics but also many citizens requesting this privilege: in March 1350, for example, two women, Annota Constabularia and Margaret Abyrnethi requested the privilege for themselves, followed in May 1350 by requests from twelve men, both clerical and lay. These mark the beginning of a long series of such requests from citizens of Dublin.[5]

Charitable giving was another way of atoning for sin and laying up treasure in the afterlife. Donations to the Church, and the establishment of churches and shrines was a common response among the wealthy of Europe's cities. Often such donations were accompanied with bequests for Masses for the dead. Was this the inspiration for the munificence of John de Grauntsete, one of Dublin's wealthiest and most prom-

inent citizens, in the autumn of 1348, some two months after
the Black Death had broken out in Dublin? In October 1348
he was granted a license to build a chapel on the stone bridge
of Dublin, most likely for the Dominicans who were probably responsible for the upkeep of the bridge, as was com-
monly the case in medieval Europe. This chapel was to be
granted:

> ...an endowment of one hundred shillings annually for the
> support of two chaplains to celebrate divine service therein
> daily for Edward III, Queen Philippa, their ancestors and suc-
> cessors, also for the welfare of the founder, the mayor, and
> commonalty of the city, and for the souls of all the faithful
> departed.

Or there is the case of John Taylor, who died in 1370 and who
in his will left the bulk of his many bequests to a wide selec-
tion of churches and chapels in Dublin and to the poor so
that Masses could be celebrated and prayers said for his soul,
his deceased parents and all the faithful departed.[6]

Going on pilgrimage was the most popular way of trying
to propitiate an angry God. Pilgrimages were important in
the life of Dublin's citizens as is indicated by the pilgrim's
badges from Rome, Canterbury and Worcester, as well as
other pilgrim-related objects that have been found during
excavations.[7] Moreover, the years immediately following the
Black Death saw an unusual number of people going on pilgrimage, not only because of the plague, but because 1350
had been designated a Holy Year. So, throughout Europe,
many set off on pilgrimage to Rome in order to avail of the
special indulgences on offer. In September 1349, the Pope

A medieval pilgrim.

mandated the Archbishop of Dublin and his suffragans to publish an indulgence that would be granted to those pilgrims who visited the Basilicas of Saints Peter and Paul and the Church of St John Lateran in Rome. Many enthusiastically made this journey. There was, for example, the Cistercian monk from St Mary's Abbey in Dublin, Thomas Wait, who in August 1350 left his monastery without permission to make the journey to Rome. Journey completed, in March 1351 he sought permission to return. Such journeys were not easy, particularly in the aftermath of the plague, and not everybody was as enthusiastic as Thomas Wait. In May 1350 the Archbishop of Dublin, for example, sought permission to make his visit to Rome every three years instead of biannually.

However, there were also various popular sites of pilgrimage in Dublin itself, by some calculations at least about thirty-five places with shrines of some kind. Christ Church Cathedral was a popular place of pilgrimage as it housed many famous relics. A list in the *Registers of Christ Church* enumerates some of these: a speaking crucifix dating from ancient times, the bones of the apostles Peter and Andrew, relics of Saints Clement, Oswald, Fide the Virgin, Wulstan, Thomas the Martyr, Edward the Confessor, Katherine, Clement, Blaise, Nicholas, Laurence, Oswald and others. It housed Ireland's most venerated relic, St Patrick's Crozier, also known as the *Baculus Jhesu* or *Bachall Íosa*, so called because according to legend it had been the staff of Christ which had been passed on to St Patrick. That this was a venerated object is suggested by an entry by Edmund Campion in his *Historie of Ireland* in 1571:

> They have been used in solemne controversies to protest and swear by St Patrick's Staffe, called Bachal esu, which oath, because upon breach thereof heavy plagues ensued, they feared more to breake than if they had sworne by the Holy Evangelist.[8]

Outside the city, there were shrines in the parish church at Finglas, in the chapels of St Begnata at Donnybrook and of St Catherine at Feldstone. Somewhat further away, but also popular with Dubliners, were the shrines of Our Lady in the Augustinian Convent at Trim and at Navan, as well as Croagh Patrick or St Patrick's Purgatory. Pilgrimages, devotions and public processions to these sites would have been a common sight in the autumn and winter of 1348.

Friar Clyn records that pilgrims of all social classes came from all over Ireland to the holy well at Thath Molyngis (see

Plate 8), now St Mullins in County Carlow, where the seventh-century monk St Moling had had a monastery and had acquired a reputation as a healer:

> In this year [1348] and particularly in the months of September and October there came together from diverse parts of Ireland, bishops and prelates, churchmen and religious, lords and others to the pilgrimage and wading of the water at Thath Molyngis, in troops and multitudes, so that you could see many thousands there at the same time for many days together. Some came from feelings of devotion but others and they the majority from dread of the plague, which then grew very rife.[9]

Needless to add, these gatherings, while serving to console a terrified population, were also ideal venues for the further transmission of plague.

As is so frequent with incomprehensible diseases, scapegoating was another common response. Instead of attributing the plague to God's anger, marginal or minority groups were blamed for instigating the plague. The 'other' became the target of people's panic. In many Continental European cities, the plague brought to the surface strains and tensions between different groups, particularly Jewish people, lepers, outsiders and foreigners, the disabled and the poor, all of whom were, in different places, considered responsible for the plague, by poisoning well water, for example. There isn't any evidence in Dublin of such scapegoating, nor of the millenarian thinking the Black Death inspired elsewhere. The absence of evidence for such responses in Dublin may be partially explained by the dearth of eyewitness accounts for the plague in Ireland in general. However, other places also did not experience the

The burning of the Jews. In various parts of Continental Europe, Jewish people were accused of causing the plague by poisoning the wells.

hysteria that characterised the plague years in many European cities. England, for example, largely escaped the excesses recorded in Continental countries; as Dr Maurice Keen writes, in words that could also be applied to Ireland, 'all seems to be in rather a minor key when it comes to reaction'. Why? The historian J.F. Lydon believes that the Irish did not have a morbid attitude to their religion, that it was not 'an oppressive nor an inhibiting factor in their lives' and that perhaps, for this reason, the medieval Irish escaped the excesses evident elsewhere. In illustrating his hypothesis, he cites Archbishop Minot of Dublin who, in reducing the number of feast days in 1367 because they were occasions of sin to the city's workers, complained that many of them never or rarely went to Mass, '...but spend almost all of the feast day or at least the greater part thereof, in taverns and drunkenness and other illicit acts of pleasure'. Since churches were also used as halls for dances, games and for storing valuables, Lydon concludes that the Irish had '...an easy familiarity with their Church which was in a very real sense the centre of their community'.[10]

Perhaps that same familiarity was also inspired by a deep-seated, almost instinctive faith that offered ways of responding to sudden death which avoided the emotional extremes and could explain the relative absence of any reference to widespread millenarian movements in post-plague Ireland. One cannot discount that a deep religious faith could have led people to accept what would have been seen as God's will. The absence of widespread hysteria could also perhaps be linked to the absence of an apocalyptic imagination in medieval Irish religion. In his study of the plague in Egypt, Michael Dols argues that the controlled reaction to plague in Islamic countries and Eastern Europe may be linked to the theology of Islam and to the absence of an apocalyptic mindset. There were no millenarian responses in Muslim society, perhaps because there is not a doctrine of the Apocalypse in orthodox Islam. Similarly, Byzantine chronicles of the Black Death do not offer any evidence of messianic movements because the Orthodox Church did not favour the *Book of Revelation* and apocalyptic ideas in general. Though apocalyptic images figure in Clyn's account of the Black Death in Ireland, they are limited and muted by contrast with those used by chroniclers elsewhere.[11]

Ireland does not seem to have escaped millenarian responses entirely, however. The Flagellants, for example, would seem to

A sixteenth-century representation of a medieval Flagellant.

have found some kind of audience in Ireland. This was a movement of lay people who, for a period of thirty-three days, pledged themselves to wandering from town to town, flagellating themselves in public with whips to atone for their sins and assuage the wrath of God. In November 1349 Pope Clement VI ordered the Archbishop of Dublin as well as the Archbishops of Armagh, Cashel and Tuam 'to warn and induce certain persons calling themselves Flagellantes to leave their vain religion'. In his communication to the Irish bishops the Pope claimed that some mendicants were responsible for encouraging the Flagellants, and most likely he had the Franciscans in mind. Some years later Archbishop Richard FitzRalph, in a sermon in Kells, County Meath on 14 May 1355, also warned against the excesses of the Flagellants. So perhaps Dublin too witnessed groups of penitents going in procession from church to church in the city, wearing white loin cloths, singing hymns and, in imitation of the Passion of Christ, beating themselves with whips until they drew blood. The authorities, both secular and ecclesiastic, viewed them with suspicion, though the public initially welcomed them. However, as their actions became ever more excessive, while yet clearly failing to halt the plague, opinion turned against them and they were outlawed. By the time we encounter references to Flagellants in Ireland, the movement was already on the wane, and if they made an appearance in Ireland, they were certainly among the last of the Flagellants. In general however, what we know of religious responses in Ireland evinced a traditionalism and sanguinity not evident in the responses to plague in Continental cities.[12]

Once infection had set in, prayer was a recourse, not simply as a form of consolation but also a possible means of healing – not surprising in a society where body and soul were seen holistically. Richard Ledrede, Bishop of Ossory during the plague years, in one of his poems reveals what would have been the attitude of many to disease; he advises that:

> …the wound of Christ's side is medicine above all others…
> For the fevered, the chilled, the withered, the dropsical,
> Cripples, paralytics, the broken-limbed, the swollen,
> Lepers, demoniacs, the desperate, the dead – it cures their every
> ill, it is the healing art for doctors.

Prayer to a favourite saint was also seen as a possible remedy and Mary, Christ's mother, was a particularly favourite intercessor during the plague. In another poem Ledrede speaks of

Mary as a healer who can 'make level what is swollen', words suggestive of skin eruptions caused by perhaps leprosy or buboes.[13]

MEDICAL AND PUBLIC HEALTH MEASURES

While God's anger was believed to be the primary cause of disease, the proximate or physical cause of the pestilence was the universal contamination of the air for which there was a number of explanations. One widely accepted explanation was that offered in 1348 by the medical faculty at the University of Paris. In a lengthy argument they attributed the plague to a conjunction on 24 March 1345 of Saturn, Jupiter and Mars in the house of Aquarius. This unusual event created changes in the atmosphere of the earth, which resulted in a corruption of the air. The corrupt air then created a malignant vapour or miasma which released poisonous fumes that entered the human body either through the skin or by breathing; these then caused an imbalance in the bodily humours and further corruption that was in turn released through the formation of buboes. This anonymous contemporary English commentator managed to synthesise a gamut of explanations:

> If I am asked what is the cause of pestilence, what is its phys-
> ical cause and by what means can someone save himself from
> it, I answer to the first question that sin is the cause. To the
> second question, I say that it arises from the sea, as the evan-
> gelist says: 'There shall be signs in the sun and in the moon and
> in the stars; and upon the earth distress of nations, by reason of

the confusion of the roaring of the sea and waves.' For the Devil, by the power committed to him when the seas rise up high, is voiding his poison, sending it forth to be added to the poison in the air, and that air spreads gradually from place to place and enters man through the ears, eyes, nose, mouth, pores and other orifices. Then, if the man has a strong constitution, nature can expel the poison through ulcers, and if the ulcers putrefy, are strangled and fully run their course, the patient will be saved, as can be clearly seen. But if the poison should be stronger than his nature, so that his constitution cannot prevail against it, then the poison instantly lays siege to the heart and the patient dies within a short time, without the relief that comes from the formation of ulcers.[14]

The transmission of disease was widely believed to occur through contagion, in the sense that it was transmitted from person to person through corrupt air. The infected body communicated its poisonous vapours to others through the breath, touch, sight or even just thought, so that pestilence was widely believed to spread directly from one person to another and one place to another. This belief allowed for some measure of human intervention. Those most likely to catch a disease were those whose temperament (superabundance of humours) or way of life (excessive eating, drinking, sexual activity and washing – activities that enlarged the pores through which contamination entered) predisposed them to disease. Many chroniclers, including Boccaccio, observed that in talking and mixing with plague victims, or in touching the clothing or possessions of the sick, the corrupt air that was lodged in the garments and possessions of victims entered the body of another person through the pores of the skin. Boccaccio describes one such event:

One day, for instance, the rags of a pauper who had died from the disease were thrown into the street, where they attracted the attention of two pigs. In their wonted fashion, the pigs first of all gave the rags a thorough mauling with their snouts after which they took them between their teeth and shook them against their cheeks. And within a short time they began to writhe as though they had been poisoned, then they both dropped dead to the ground, spreadeagled upon the rags that had brought about their undoing.

Friar Clyn too emphasizes the contagious nature of the plague and notes that those who even touched victims were also infected and died. Fearing contamination, people were loath to visit the sick or bury the dead. Clearly then, even though the precise cause of the plague was not understood, there was a widespread acceptance that it was contagious, not in the modern sense, but in the sense that it was a disease which could spread from person to person by exhalation.[15]

The most-often cited advice offered in order to avoid contagion was the very practical advice to flee contaminated areas: *fugere cito, longe, et tarde reverti* (flee quickly and far, return slowly), even though flight was also seen as an avoidance of God's will, an act of treachery and cowardice. Clearly this was a response that was possible for the upper classes such as the protagonists of the *Decameron*, but for the poor it was not an option. This response would continue to be popular into the succeeding centuries: in the fifteenth century, for example, Bengt Knutsson, a Swedish bishop, in his plague commentary, which was based on a popular fourteenth-century plague tract, wrote:

...pestilence sores are contagious because of infectious humours, and the reek or smoke of such sores is venomous and corrupts the air. And therefore one should flee such persons as are infected. In pestilence time nobody should stand in a great press of people because some man among them may be infected.[16]

In other European cities, the wealthier and more influential citizens fled as soon as there was news of an impending plague. Wealthy Dubliners would flee the city during later outbreaks of plague in the fifteenth and sixteenth centuries. Many may have abandoned the city in 1348 also, though the difficulty of travelling overland, given the threats from the surrounding Gaelic-Irish, would have prevented any huge exodus.

Other preventative measures were many and varied, all centered on the notion that contaminated air had to be kept at bay. Corrupt air was, above all, signalled by its smell, which played an important role in the semiology of pestilence. Doctors advised people to avoid dwellings located near stinking places and stagnant waters, to ensure rooms were ventilated by northerly winds, to avoid the southerly pestilence-bearing winds, to use herbs and aromatic plants as smelling salts and air purifiers, and to light fires in order to banish the stink from houses and cities. Those treating the ill were warned to avoid the gaze of the patient, as even that alone could transmit plague. Heat and warmth were also seen as defences and so people were recommended to light fires, even in the middle of summer. It could have been an effective measure, in fact, as heat can destroy the plague bacillus. People were also advised to strengthen the natural heat of the body by drinking good wine and by moderate exercise. Finally, what perhaps one might call the power of positive thinking was highly prized as a deterrent

The doctor's visit.

against plague. On the theory that contentment helped achieve a balance in the body's humours, the English poet, Lydgate, advised the man who '…would resiste the strok of pestilence/Let him be glad, and voide al hevynesse'.[17]

During outbreaks of epidemics, concern was also focused on what were believed to be other sources or agents of contamination, such as lepers. Though leprosy had already declined by the beginning of the fourteenth century, nevertheless with the outbreak of plague measures were enacted against lepers – not necessarily because they were scapegoats, but because they were believed to foul the air and thus spread the disease. The advent of the Great Plague led to many anti-leprosy measures elsewhere also. For example, in 1347-1348 the King ordered all lepers to leave the city of London and similar measures were passed in Nottingham. Dublin, too, had its population of lepers. From the early fourteenth century, the authorities in the city had decreed that lepers were not to be allowed within the city's walls, and anybody found sheltering them was to be fined or imprisoned. Instead they were expected to go to hospitals outside the walls. A number of hospitals catered for lepers: St Stephen's on the site of the present Mercer's Hospital; St James' Hospital at the Steyne, later known as the Steine Hospital or *lazaretto* on Lazar's Hill; St Lawrence's in Palmerstown, which was run by the Knights Hospitallers; and a home for lepers in Leperstown (the present Leopardstown), which at some point was also used as a quarantine station for pilgrims to Dublin. It is very likely that these leper houses were used for plague victims during the Black Death. In certain other places we know that plague victims were removed to leper houses outside city limits, and so *lazaretto* came to mean a plague hospital.[18]

Once infected with plague, medical remedies were few and foundering. Medicine in Ireland in the fourteenth century, as in the rest of Europe, was dominated by Arabic scholastic medicine. Many scholarly medical manuscripts have been discovered, most of which are fifteenth-century translations of work written elsewhere. *Rosa Anglica*, a fourteenth-century work by John of Gaddesden, a doctor in the royal court, was widely used in Ireland in the fifteenth century. The texts of the twelfth-century Renaissance, the works of Galen, Avicenna and Hippocrates, have survived, as well as some fifty-eight translations of late thirteenth and fourteenth-century works, indicating their widespread use. All propose theories regarding the causes and treatment of disease. In practice, however, medicine was a mixture of knowledge gleaned from medical texts, superstition, moralizing and religious faith with the addition of some folk medicine and homeopathic remedies, as is evidenced in a medieval Irish manuscript written by one doctor:

> May the merciful God have mercy on us all. I have collected practical notes from several works for the honour of God, for the benefit of the Irish people, for the instruction of any pupil and for the love of my friends and of my kindred. I have translated from Latin into Gaelic, from the authority of Galen, in the last book of his *Practical Pantheon* and from the book of *Prognostics* of Hippocrates. These are things, gentle, sweet and profitable, and of little evil, things which have often been tested by us and by our instructors. I pray God to bless those doctors who will use this book, and I lay it on their souls, as an injunction, that they extract the practical rules (herein contained) and more especially, that they do their duty devotedly in cases where they receive no pay. Moreover let him not be in mortal sin, and let him implore the patient to be also free from grievous sin. Let him offer up a secret prayer for the sick person, and implore the Heavenly Father, the Physician and Balm-Giver of all mankind to prosper the work he is entering upon.[19]

Hospital was intended primarily for the elderly poor, for lepers, and occasionally for the dying, but not for the ill. Besides those hospitals founded for the care of lepers, there were other hospitals and infirmaries, most of which cared for the poor. Dublin, in fact, seems to have looked after its poor well and other testimony, such as some contemporary poetry, indicates that awareness of their plight of the poor was acutely developed in Ireland. There was an infirmary in the Priory of Holy Trinity at Christ Church run by the Augustinian canons. The largest and most well-known was the hospital for the poor and for orphans in the Priory of St John the Baptist outside the New Gate, run by the Crutched Friars, known as Palmer's Hospital, or the 'poor hospital of St John without New Gate'. By the mid-fourteenth century the hospital had 155 people in its care.[20]

The treatment of illness was in the hands not only of the monastic orders but also of physicians and herbalists of whom we know little, especially in Ireland. Some medical prescrip-

A medieval apothecary.

tions inscribed on slates were found in County Louth, which date from the early fifteenth century, but none deals with plague. Theories regarding the diagnosis and treatment of disease in general varied. The medicinal virtues of herbs and minerals are frequently mentioned. When, for example, the Prior of Holy Trinity fell ill in 1346, he was treated with a rose water and sugar mixture – rose water as it was considered to have cooling qualities against fever. In the aftermath of the plague, rose water was also recommended as a protective measure to all those who came into contact with plague victims. Herbs and plants were widely used as plague deterrents or cures; Erasmus, for example, had a cornucopia of possible remedies growing in his garden. Another common procedure in treating plague was bloodletting, which had been used since the time of Galen to alleviate plague and was warmly advocated in 1347 by the Medical Faculty of Paris. The belief was that the procedure cooled the body, quenched fever and released poisons or harmful humours, thereby preventing them from reaching the heart. A fifteenth-century treatise on plague from England describes the procedure in this way:

> During the pestilence everyone over seven should be made to vomit daily from an empty stomach, and twice a week, or more often if necessary, he should lie well wrapped up in a warm bed and drink warm ale with ginger so that he sweats copiously… And as soon as he feels an itch or prickling in his flesh he must use a goblet or cupping horn to let blood and draw down the blood from the heart. And this should be done two or three times at intervals of one or two days at most. And if he should feel himself oppressed deep within the body,

then he should let blood in the nearest veins, either in the arms or in the main veins of the feet.

It was a remedy against plague highly recommended by John of Gaddesden in his *Rosa Anglica* that was widely used in Ireland, and it is therefore perhaps not a coincidence that a number of Irish manuscripts contain a late fourteenth-century poem entitled *On Bloodletting*. The procedure was still used in London in the seventeenth century and even as late as 1834 during an epidemic in Egypt.[21]

However, in 1348 medical lore in general was severely tested by the bubonic plague and led to all sorts of exotic remedies being suggested, such as the following from John of Burgundy's treatise of 1365:

Let the patient be given this confection, which strengthens the heart, expels harmful flatulence from it and quenches fever. Take conserves of violets, roses, bugloss, borage and oranges, powdered roses and sandalwood, cold tragacanth, an electuary of the three sandalwoods, powder to encourage moistness, a cold electuary, camphor and candied roses, mix them together without applying heat and place them in a box, and if the patient is of a hot complexion, or if the fever is intense, add six or seven grains of camphor. If the patient is rich and can afford it, pearls, gold leaf, pure silver, jacinths, emeralds, and the bone from the heart of a stag should be added.

Such treatments continued to be used into the nineteenth century. A record of 1804 from Smyrna noted that plague patients were rubbed with warm oil and put in a room

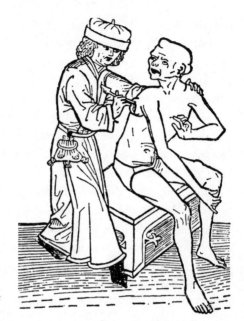

A doctor pierces a patient's buboes in this 1482 print from Nuremberg.
The procedure was intended to allow the 'pestilential' matter to escape and thus to save the patient.

warmed by a pan of coals in which various perfumes were thrown, causing the patient to sweat. This treatment, if continued for several days, was reported as highly successful in effecting cures.[22]

On a societal level many cities on the European mainland took various practical measures to stem the spread of plague, focusing on those very aspects of public sanitation that had for long been a continuing concern. The air was fumigated with strong-smelling perfumes, the streets cleared of pigs, wild dogs and rubbish, the clothing of victims burned and, the most controversial gesture of all, *cordons sanitaires* imposed around towns. A few cities, such as Venice, refused admission to ships and people carrying plague, and hospitals were set up outside the city. In particular, extreme care was taken with the burial of the dead, and once the numbers outstripped the usual burial places, the dead were buried in mass graves and pits. In Tournai, for example, the chronicler Gilbert li Muisis tells of extensive measures taken in the wake of the plague's outbreak: graves had to be dug six feet deep; post-funeral gatherings in the houses of the dead were forbidden; only the father, brother or husband of the deceased were to be allowed wear mourning garments. A few months later as the plague continued to rage, this prohibition was extended further – nobody was allowed wear mourning clothes, bells were not to be rung, bodies could not be laid out in churches and only two could accompany the funeral. Similar measures were adopted in Florence, Pistoia and Gloucester.[23] The fear was not only of public panic but also that the dead bodies would generate further corruption in the air. To what extent Dublin's authorities introduced such measures is not known, but given their earlier noted concerns with hog sties, smells and contamination, clearly the authorities took responsibility for public health. It is therefore most likely that in the immediate aftermath of the plague's outbreak they undertook measures similar to those adopted elsewhere. In 1366, for example, a grant of customs was made not only for murage and paving the streets, but also for the cleaning of the streets and lanes. An order in the same year forbade the slaughter of cattle within the city's walls, in order to prevent 'the excessive and noxious stenches hitherto caused by slaughter of cattle in the city'.[24]

However, further outbreaks of the plague had to occur before cities learned to develop effective and consistent public health responses. Eventually, towns everywhere learned from the experience of the Black Death. Italian cities pointed the way by establishing health boards to enforce special measures for controlling epidemic disease. During later outbreaks of plague, temporary plague hospitals, or *lazarettos* were erected outside the walls of the city to isolate suspected plague victims. This was to be the response adopted in cities throughout Europe in later centuries. So, authorities responded in the best possible way in accordance with the best knowledge of disease at the time. However, a catastrophe such as plague tested all the resources of medical men and city officials, because the disease was not understood. Even a century later plague in Dublin was still being attributed to 'pestilential exhalations' in the air and the miasmatic theory would continue to dominate medical thinking until the later nineteenth century.[25]

BEHAVIOURAL REACTIONS

What kind of effect did such a tragedy have on people's behaviour and psyche? Contemporary chroniclers everywhere emphasize – perhaps formulaically – that the plague caused a disruption in people's normal behaviour and values, famously compared by an American sociologist to the experience of the 'Lost Generation' after the First World War.[26] Often cited are the breakdown of the normal ties of family and kinship as people, afraid of catching the disease, avoided all contact with victims. Boccaccio's testimony is typical of many such accounts:

It was not merely a question of one citizen avoiding another, and of people almost invariably neglecting their neighbours and rarely or never visiting their relatives, addressing them only from a distance; this scourge had implanted so great a terror in the hearts of men and women that brothers abandoned brothers, uncles their nephews, sisters their brothers, and in many cases wives their husbands. But even worse, and almost incredible, was the fact that fathers and mothers refused to nurse and assist their own children, as though they didn't belong to them.

In Siena, Agnolo di Tura wrote that the dead were left unburied or thrown into pits so poorly covered that the dogs gnawed their bones. However, not all human feeling was completely lost; he adds:

> And I, Agnolo di Tura, called the Fat, buried my five children with my own hands, and so did many others likewise ... So many died that everyone thought that the end of the world had come.

And in Scotland, John of Fordun in his *Scotichronicon*, wrote that the plague:

> ...generated such horror that children did not dare to visit their dying parents, or parents their children, but fled for fear of contagion as if from leprosy or a serpent.

Friar Clyn also speaks, albeit more soberly, of the fear and horror that so affected people that they '... hardly dared to perform works of piety and mercy; that is, visiting the sick and burying the dead'. However, the high mortality figures Clyn cited for the mendicant friars in Dublin indicate that they at least cannot have shirked performing works of piety and mercy. The fear of burying the dead, as well as other factors, led elsewhere to mass, open-pit graves where the dead were piled unceremoniously and quickly in layers. One chronicle describes what happened in Florence:

At every church they dug deep pits down to the water level; and thus those who were poor who died during the night were bundled up quickly and thrown into the pit. In the morning when a large number of bodies were found in the pit, they took some earth and shovelled it down on top of them; and later others were placed on top of them and then another layer of earth, just as one makes lasagne with layers of pasta and cheese.

Burying the dead in Tournai. Li Muisis, *Antiquitates Flandriae*.

Archaeologists have yet to identify any such pit graves in Dublin from the time of the Black Death. However, there is evidence of mass burials in the medieval period as pit graves have been uncovered which date to some time between the late twelfth and the mid-fourteenth century. One such grave with six skeletons was found in the Temple Bar area, at 3-4 Crow Street, which was the site of an Augustinian friary. Another mass grave was discovered during excavations in Swords, one of the manors of the Archbishop of Dublin in the Middle Ages, which has been dated to the late thirteenth or early fourteenth century. Here six bodies, females and infants, were thrown on top of one another, evidence of a hasty burial. This, together with the fact that they were not buried in the cemetery that more than likely was attached to a monastery nearby, suggests that they were victims of pestilence or some other trauma. Clearly then, mass graves were not unknown in medieval Ireland, and if Clyn's mortality figures are in any way accurate, then special plague cemeteries may well have been created in Dublin and in surrounding villages to deal with the unusual demand.[27]

The crisis engendered by the Black Death elicited the gamut of human responses to be expected in the face of sudden and widespread death. The English chronicler Knighton, among others, tells us that in the aftermath of the catastrophe people did not care any more about wealth or possessions, with the result that prices fell everywhere. But that was likely a short-term reaction, limited to a few. Contemporary chronicles repeatedly emphasize the decadence and vice prevalent in the post-plague era and the complete abandonment of normal restraints.[28]

According to Boccaccio, some people responded to the horror of the plague by drinking and carousing and enjoying life to the full, though this pursuit of pleasure was also seen as having a therapeutic effect in helping to balance the body's humours.

Unfortunately, medieval Ireland has no Boccaccio, and we have to rely principally on ecclesiastical records to get a sense of people's behaviour. That church officials had become concerned with the level of violence in society is suggested by a

Ebrietas et Luxus. Carousing in time of plague: a way of maintaining a balance in the body's humours and thereby keeping the plague at bay – or an instance of *carpe diem?*

Papal letter of 1359 giving the Archbishop of Dublin permission to pardon clerks and laymen who had been excommunicated for 'taking part in the destruction of churches, towns and other places, burnings, slayings of ecclesiastics and public spoilations'. A further Papal order in 1373 decreed a yearly meeting of a council which would 'draw up statutes for the reformation of the life and manners of clergy and people'. Most of the surviving evidence in Ireland focuses on an increase in greed and injustice. Richard Ledrede, Bishop of Ossory, in one of his Latin poems begs for Christ's mercy and redemption since:

> *Avarice increases, deception and malice,*
> *Love and justice are in flight from our land,*
> *Everywhere rapine flourishes, hatred and arson.*

Other poems from the mid-fourteenth century decry the prevalence of greed, dishonesty, cheating and abuse of power at all levels of society, always at the expense of the poor. This too echoes experiences recorded elsewhere. The contemporary French chronicler, Jean de Venette, emphasises the increase in greed, miserliness and quarrelsomeness after the Black Death, and this despite the fact that the survivors were better off than they had ever been.[29]

Survivors attempted to profit from the turmoil to increase their own holdings and possessions. Marchione di Coppo Stefani, in his chronicle on the plague in Florence, for example writes about people plundering the houses of those who had died. After the pestilence ended in September 1348,

> people began to return to look after their houses and possessions. And there were so many houses full of goods with-

out a master that it was stupefying. Then those who would inherit these goods began to appear. And such it was that those who had nothing found themselves rich with what did not seem to be theirs and they were unseemly because of it. Women and men began to dress ostentatiously.

This tallies also with the testimony of Matteo Villani who shortly after the plague wrote of Florence:

The common people by reason of the abundance and super-fluity that they found would no longer work at their accustomed trades; they wanted the dearest and most delicate foods …while children and common women clad themselves in all the fair and costly garments of the illustrious who had died.[30]

This then is the context for the complaints voiced by Archbishop FitzRalph of Armagh in the thirty-one surviving sermons that he delivered between 1348-1349 and 1351-1356. Though these particularly address conditions in Drogheda, those pertaining in Dublin, a similar port city, cannot have differed significantly. People's wickedness and ignorance is a constant theme in the sermons he delivered between 1348 and 1355. In the five sermons he gave soon after his arrival around April 1348 and before the outbreak of the Black Death, he focused on the themes of usury, temptation, sin (lust, avarice, lack of charity), the necessity of penance, reparation, restitution and prayer. Then in a sermon on 25 March 1349, the first he delivered after the plague had broken out, he contrasted the sinless state of Mary, the mother of Jesus, with the injustice and dishonesty of his listeners. He then left Ireland for a while and, on his return in 1351, his sermons continued to emphasize man's sinfulness and the necessity for confession, restitution and contrition, and he harked frequently on the vanity of possessions and the sinfulness of hoarding wealth. He castigated people's growing concern with property and profit, not surprisingly in the post-plague context where the pickings were all the greater for the survivors. In a charge that addressed what was elsewhere a common occurrence in the wake of the Black Death, he condemned those who interfered with the inheritance rights of women and minors.

In general, contemporaries emphasize the growing selfishness and lack of charity among the rich and the faithful, a phenomenon that had immediate repercussions in the cities, which relied so much for their upkeep on the donations of the rich. To what extent such complaints were affected by the Black Death is a debatable point. Many contemporaries agreed with the French chronicler, Jean de Venette, who wrote, 'from that time charity began to grow cold'. In many of his sermons Archbishop FitzRalph also voiced a concern for the more vulnerable in society and repeatedly chastised the wealthy for neglecting their social obligations, and for not distributing their superfluous wealth. He emphasised, perhaps not always objectively, the lack of charity evident in people's dealings with each other, and especially with the Church. At the opening of a synod in 1352, he complained that in his diocese were '… many usurers, many perjurers, many hostile to the church and priests'. He was troubled by the lack of charity among wealthy merchants and by their tendency to postpone charitable giving until after death. Post-mortem giving, he argued, wasn't as meritorious as giving during life. FitzRalph's problem was compounded by the fact that what charity was being given was going largely to the mendicant orders and especially the Franciscans, who were particularly popular everywhere, especially as confessors.[31]

The fall-off in donations, of course, may have been occasioned simply by the fact that there were fewer donors after the plague. However, some historians argue that the Black Death generally had the effect of heightening intolerance towards the poor, partly because of the improved position of the labourer, both rural and urban, in the post-plague era, and partly because of the dwindling of landlords' discretionary income. In Dublin, for example, there aren't any records of new hospitals being founded in the post-plague era. Moreover, the increasingly vociferous complaints about beggars suggest a growing intolerance. Ecclesiastics too are increasingly being accused of greed and self-interest. In 1363 the Prior of the Hospital of St John the Baptist near Dublin was charged with misusing and misappropriating the wealth and property of the institution, to the detriment of the men, women and orphans being cared for there. In 1364 the hospitals and pious places in Dublin had neglected the 'duty of charity' to such an extent that the pope ordered the Archbishop of Dublin to revoke their constitutions and privileges. Studies in England and elsewhere indicate a clear decline in charitable giving. In *Les Pauvres au Moyen Âge*, Michel Mollat argues that charitable giving and charitable institutions declined after the Black Death. Christopher Dyer in his study of standards of living in the later medieval period agrees that after 1350 people exhibited increasing intolerance of the poor and an increasing reluctance to fund any charitable institutions. Other historians would see the change as coming later. Dr P.H. Callum, while concurring in the fact of a decline in charitable giving, disagrees about its timing. He argues that in fact there was an increase in the number of hospitals and charitable institutions after the Black Death, and that only in the later fifteenth century did attitudes begin to change. He also contends that if there was a decline, it took place not after the Black Death but at the beginning of the century, in the wake of the 1315-1318 famine when the extent of suffering led to 'compassion fatigue'.[32]

Charges of immorality in general are increasingly levelled against the clergy in the post-plague era. Widespread mortality and the consequent despair have been cited as the cause of a general decline in moral standards among the clergy everywhere. In England, the poet William Langland castigated the clergy for their greed and dereliction of duty:

> Then I heard parish priests complaining to the Bishop that since the Plague their parishes were too poor to live in; so they asked permission to live in London, where they could traffic in Masses, and chime their voices to the sweet jingling of silver.

What sources there are seem to warrant the conclusion that the clergy in Ireland evinced the same behaviour as their European counterparts. Increasing numbers of clerics seek permission to live elsewhere, usually in England, while yet drawing the proceeds from their benefices in Dublin. The practice of pluralism also grew apace. While the Black Death did not create such practices, increasing lay criticism of the moral habits of the clergy after 1348 would seem to suggest that the plague intensified clerical abuses, or at least made the public less willing to tolerate them. Some of these complaints were voiced in the sermons of Archbishop FitzRalph.

1 *Xenopsylla cheopis*, the plague-carrying flea, here shown engorged with blood.

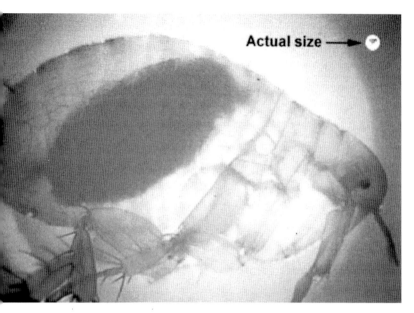

2 Dalkey, according to Friar Clyn, was one of the port towns where the Black Death first appeared in 1348. During the plague of 1575, Dalkey Island, pictured here, was a refuge for Dubliners fleeing the plague in the city.

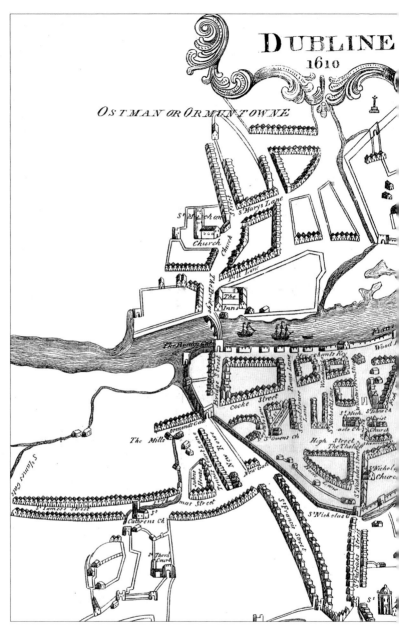

3 Speed's Map of Dublin, from his *Theatre of the Empire of Great Britain* (1611).
The earliest known map of Dublin, it depicts the city as a compact, walled settlement with some streets branching out from the centre.

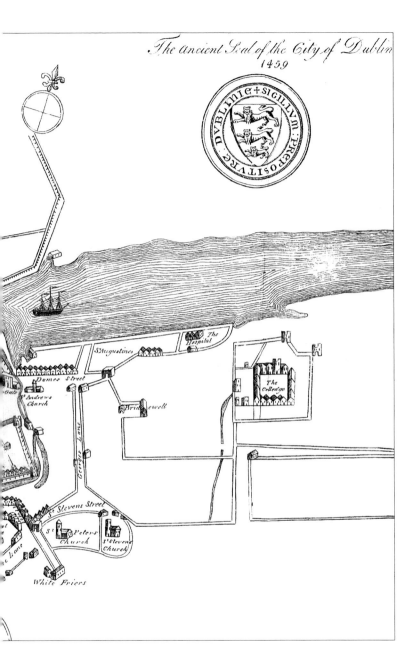

DVBLINIE + SIGILLVM : PRE POSITVRE

The Hospital

S.t Augustines

The Colledge

Dames Street

S.t Andrews Church

Gate

Bridewell

George Lane

S.t Stevens Street

S.t Peters Church

S.t Stevens Church

Lane

White Friers

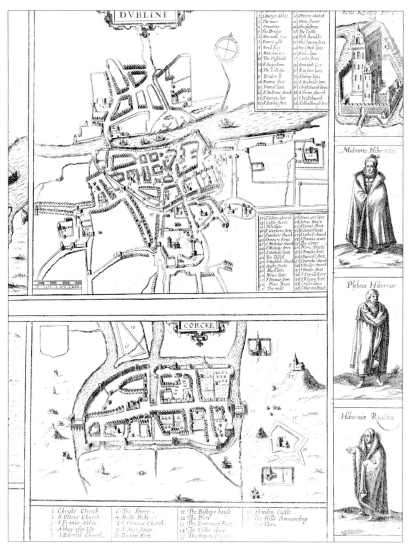

4 Dublin City, from the first published collection of plans and views of cities.
Braun and Hogenberg, *Civitates Orbis Terrarum*, vol. 1 (1572).

5 Howth – one of the harbours through which the plague entered Ireland, according to Friar Clyn. In the foreground is the church of St Mary's Abbey. Nearby is Lambay Island, which is home to the last remaining colony of black rats in Ireland.

6 This page: Cage-House. Timber-framed houses, such as this, were a feature of medieval Dublin. The last cage-work house was demolished in 1812. Joyce in *Ulysses* describes medieval Dublin as 'the starving cagework city'.

7 *Opposite above*: St Audoen's Lane, connecting High Street and Cook Street; this lane was once lined with post-and-wattle houses; '…more people died in the outskirts and in narrow lanes than in broad streets and market-places'. (Gilbert li Muisis, *Antiquitates Flandriae*).

8: *Opposite*: Thath Molyngis (in St. Mullins, Co. Carlow): 'In this year [1348] and particularly in the months of September and October there came together from diverse parts of Ireland, bishops and prelates, churchmen and religious, lords and others to the pilgrimage and wading of the water at Thath Molyngis, in troops and multitudes, so that you could see many thousands there at the same time for many days together. Some came from feelings of devotion but others and they the majority from dread of the plague, which then grew very rife.'
Friar Clyn, *Annals of Ireland*.

9 Reliquary of the heart of Archbishop St Lawrence O'Toole, who died in 1189, in Christ Church Cathedral. According to legend, his heart was brought back in an iron cask to Dublin in 1230 from Normandy where he had been buried.

10 *Left:* Contemporary Italian representation of Mary, Mother of Mercy, and protector against the plague. Outside the city's walls is the skeletal, winged figure of Death pursuing a young family fleeing the city, but the Archangel Raphael stands ready to strike Death.

12 *Opposite below:* Christ Church Cathedral. Founded c.1038, it was transferred to the Canons Regular of St Augustine about 1163. The medieval cathedral was completed around 1240. The small public park in front was once the site of the Augustinian Priory of Holy Trinity. The present cathedral is largely a nineteenth-century restoration, though its crypt is the oldest medieval building in Dublin.

11 Medieval Dublin: A City of Churches. Here, St Michael's Church (now home to Dublinia Heritage Centre), with Christ Church Cathedral in the foreground. St Michael's, one of the smallest churches in the city, became a parish in 1447.

13 St Audoen's Church, the only remaining medieval parish church in Dublin. It was founded by the Normans and dedicated to the Norman saint, Audoen of Rouen. It was one of the largest parishes in the city and was associated in the Middle Ages with a group of guilds. The doorway and parts of the nave date to the thirteenth century.

14 Squint windows, St Audoen's. According to legend, these were intended for lepers who were not allowed within churches, or in some instances even within the walls of a medieval city. More likely however, the windows enabled priests living in the adjacent house to view the high altar.

16 *Opposite below:* Four Courts, formerly the Dominican Priory of St Saviour's. The Dominicans came to Dublin in 1224 and built their monastery on land between Church Street and Chancery Lane, roughly the area occupied today by the Four Courts. The monastery was burned by the citizens in 1315 in an attempt to halt the advance of the Bruces on the city and to provide stones for the repairing of the city walls. It was subsequently rebuilt, but was suppressed in 1539. In 1581 the King's Inns, lodgings for lawyers, was established on the site.

5 St Patrick's Cathedral. An early Christian site on which the Normans built a cathedral in 1191. The medieval cathedral was constructed in the first half of the thirteenth century and was the biggest church in medieval Ireland. It was reconstructed and restored in the nineteenth century. Its resident clergy were severely affected by the Black Death.

17 St Audoen's Gate – one of the medieval gates on the northern side of the city's wall and the only surviving gateway of the medieval city.

18 The medieval wall of Dublin – the only remaining section of the wall whose upkeep taxed the hard-pressed citizens of post-plague Dublin.

19 A section of the reconstructed medieval wall of Dublin.

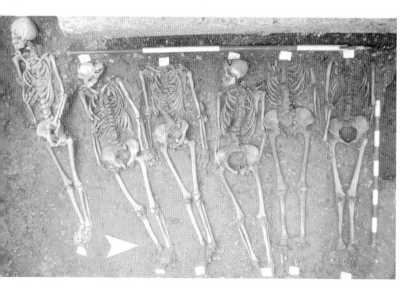

20 Detail from mass burial graves from the site of the former Royal Mint at East Smithfield in London.

21 Detail from mass burial graves from the site of the former Royal Mint at East Smithfield in London.

22 Constructed in the 1450s, the double-effigy tomb of Margaret Jenico and her husband, Roland FitzEustace, Baron of Portlester (died 1496), in St Audoen's Church.

23 The Rice tomb in Waterford is typical of a type that became increasingly common in the Dublin area in the fifteenth century. The top slab is covered with the effigy of an emaciated cadaver; the sides feature the apostles and saints. The inscription includes the classic *memento mori* phrases: '…Whoever you may be, passerby, stop, weep as you read. I am what you are going to be, and I was what you are. I beg of you, pray for me! It is our lot to pass through the jaws of death. Lord Christ, we beg of thee, we implore thee, be merciful to us! Thou who has come to redeem the lost condemn not the redeemed' (Rae, 774)

24 Beaulieu Cadaver. A cadaver tombstone from Beaulieu churchyard in Slane, Co. Meath, one of the more realistic examples of late medieval cadaver tombstones.

25 St Mary's Abbey. A Cistercian abbey founded in 1139, possibly on the site of an older church, and one of the wealthiest and most important religious establishments in medieval Ireland. It had a harbour of its own on the river and its own market, and it was the centre of one of the suburbs that grew up outside the city's walls. Following the dissolution of the monasteries during the Reformation, it was used as a stable, a munitions dump and a quarry, until it was demolished in 1676. Today, little remains except for the Chapter House in Meeting-House Lane as well as a sixteenth century statue of the Virgin and Child.

26 Trinity College: once the site of a pesthouse. In the Middle Ages, the Augustinian Priory of All Saints or All Hallows was located here. After the Reformation it was granted to Dublin Corporation in 1538, by a King grateful for the city's loyalty during the rebellion of Silken Thomas Fitzgerald.

In one sermon in 1352 he accused the clergy of fornication, adultery, marriage, nepotism, gluttony, drunkenness, hypocrisy and greed, and in sermon after sermon inveighed against their lack of spiritual motivation. The decrees of the synod of Armagh in 1383 bear ample testimony to a Church riddled with abuse, at least by official Vatican standards: decrees against the oppression of the Church, the sale of ecclesiastical offices to lay persons, the irresponsibility of the clergy, the keeping of harlots and concubines by priests, and more. The declining fortunes of the hospital of St John the Baptist in Dublin were not helped by the trial in 1441 of its Prior, James Cotyl, on charges of being 'a public fornicator who had begotten children'.[33] The author of the fifteenth-century Irish tract, *Salus populi* bewailed the times when 'persons of ye church covet more to plough   with ye plough rusticall than with ye plough apostiall' and goes on to complain that:

> the prelates of the Church and the clergy is much cause of all the disorder of the land; for there is no archbishop, ne bishop, ne prior, parson, ne vicar, ne any other person of the Church, high or low, great or small, English or Irish that useth to preach the word of God, saving the poor friars beggars.

However, another contemporary writer didn't share this admiration of the mendicant friars and vents his sarcastic remarks about the brazenly beggaring Franciscans and the proud and arrogant Dominicans. Nor did he spare the monks. In a poem entitled *Satire*, he mocks:

> *…ye holy monks with your corrin,*
> *Late and early filled with ale and wine!*
> *Deep can ye booze, that is all your care*

He is equally caustic on the subject of priests: '… ye priests with your broad books/Though your crowns be shaven, fair be your crooks' – and clearly had little respect for the nuns of St Mary's Abbey who, fond of their comfort and oblivious to their vows of poverty, wear shoes.[34]

The criticism of the clergy and especially of the mendicants had further repercussions in that clearly the number of new entrants to religious houses in Dublin fell in the later fourteenth century. Even the mendicant orders, which were recruiting widely in the western dioceses of Ireland, suffered in the Dublin area. From 1400 to 1508 only four new houses of mendicant friars were founded in the Archdiocese of Dublin, by contrast with forty in the Archdiocese of Tuam, twenty-eight in Armagh and eighteen in Cashel. This decline may have been due to an absolute decline in the number of young men – here, the fact that the plague particularly affected towns in the east and that some of the later outbreaks particularly affected children and the young is of significance. In the west of Ireland, by contrast with the area around Dublin, an increasing number of friaries sprang up. However, one cannot discount the effect of the charges of greed and worldliness made about the religious orders in the wake of the plague. These charges may not always have been deserved of course. They arose partly in response to a Papal order of 1350 that had granted the Franciscans special privileges with regard to preaching, hearing confession and burial rights, all of which threatened the position of the secular clergy and were seen by some bishops as interfering with the running of their dioceses. Nevertheless, criticism of the friars was widespread. The contemporary English chronicler, John of Reading, commenting on similar developments in England, pointed to the plague as the origin of the decline of the mendicant ideal:

> The mammon of iniquity wounded the regular clergy very much, but wounded the mendicants fatally. The superfluous wealth poured their way, through confessions and bequests, in such quantities that they scarcely condescended to accept oblations. Forgetful of their profession and rule, which imposed total poverty and mendicancy, they lusted after things of the world and of the flesh, not of heaven.[35]

PSYCHOLOGICAL AND ARTISTIC RESPONSES

One of the most hotly contested questions regarding contemporary responses to the Black Death is whether or not it brought about a paradigmatic shift in people's perception of their world. The English historian, G.R. Owst, wrote that in the later medieval world, 'the shock of death, with the yet greater tragedy that might be in store beyond it, cast its shadow backward athwart the whole of human life'. Artistic works particularly are often cited as evidence that gloom, pessimism and cynicism took hold of the European mind. Historians, most notably Millard Meiss in the influential *Painting in Florence and Siena after the Black Death*, have credited the Black Death with inducing a radical change in the way medieval people thought about their world and lives, principally in an increasing concern with suffering and death, and in an obsession with the macabre. It has become a cliché to refer to the increasing despair and death-bound thinking evident in late fourteenth-century art. In the memorable words of Huizinga:

> No other epoch has laid so much stress as the expiring Middle Ages on the thought of death. An everlasting call of *memento mori* resounds through life …The medieval soul demands the concrete embodiment of the perishable: that of the putrefying corpse.

However, one must emphasize that the interest in the macabre and the consciousness of death did not begin in the fourteenth

Contemporary representations of death: *Death felling the Tree of Life.*

Contemporary representations of death: *Dance of death.*

century. As Dr Paul Binksi notes, 'the penitential world of the late Middle Ages is in a sense no more than a magnificent foot-note to St Augustine and the Fathers of the Church'.[36]

Nevertheless, the fact that the darker, more penitential world of Christianity was foregrounded at this time had much to do with circumstances at the end of the fourteenth century, as the impact of continual outbreaks of plague heightened people's awareness of suffering and death. It is not surprising that, faced with the continuing deaths of family and neigh-bours, people's thinking came to be dominated by thoughts of dying. Understandably, texts such as *Meditationes Vitae Christi,* with its vivid images of Christ's suffering, became widely popular among people themselves too used to suffering and seeking some transcendence. This came to be a popular text in Ireland in the following century and was translated as *Smaointe Beatha Chríostí*. So too images of a suffering human Christ are emphasized in the few surviving late fourteenth-century Irish crucifixes which depict Christ as a man in pain, with a pronounced ribcage, hollow stomach and drooping head.[37]

Another way in which people's preoccupation with death found expression was in their burial practices. Perhaps as a reaction to the mass graves and hasty burials of the plague era, people became increasingly concerned with the choice of cemetery and funeral memorials, though this concern was confined to the wealthy townspeople who could afford such elaboration. Dr S.K. Cohn writes:

> ...the turning point in this attention to precise burial places was the Black Death of 1348 and its return in 1362-3. Perhaps out of fear of mass ignominious burial, testators became less content to leave the places and preparations for their final remains solely to the discretion of executives, confrères, parish priests, or even next of kin.

After the Black Death in cities such as London, Douai (Flanders) and in the cities of Tuscany and Umbria, people increasingly specified their desired burial place in their wills: the percentage climbed from less than 20% before the plague to over 90% in Umbria and 50% in Douai after 1348. There are an increasing number of instances of testators leaving precise instructions for the adornment of altars, vestments for priests, even the building of a family burial chapel and vault.

As the plague of 1348 was succeeded by subsequent plagues, requests became ever more precise and elaborate, as did arrangements for memorial Masses. For example, numbers were chosen for their religious symbolic significance – five for the five wounds of Christ, four for the four evangelists, twelve for the apostles. These practices are echoed in Dublin where a number of rich men in their wills left money for Masses, as well as for food and drink to be distributed to the poor of the city. In 1440, for example, Richard Donogh left 'five pounds of wax to make five large candles to be placed around his corpse at wake and funeral' and 6s 8d 'for bread and ale on the night of his wake and day of burial, to be distributed to the poor'. The recipients were no doubt expected in return to pray for his soul.[38]

The style of funerary monuments changed also, and the Black Death was surely a factor in the new fashions in funerary sculpture that developed in the Dublin area as well as in Meath and Kilkenny in the mid-fifteenth century. A shift becomes evident, away from the simple, uninscribed and unadorned tombs common in the earlier Middle Ages to more ornate mensa tombs in the fifteenth century. Perhaps here, more than in any other area is the pervasive consciousness of death most evident, as the sides of tombs were inscribed with weepers and details of the deceased. These kinds of tombs became particularly popular in the Dublin area in the mid-fifteenth century, and examples survive in St Audoen's Church and in St Mary's Abbey in Howth. In later tombs – the so-called apostle tombs – the weepers are depicted as the apostles, as if the world of the spirit had also been invaded by the sorrow of death. One might argue that these new tombs emphasize the finality and human pathos of death, more than had been the case in tombs of earlier times: death is portrayed more as an end of a human's life than the beginning of a new life, and the emphasis is on grieving.

Of course, one may not discount the fact that this change may simply have been due to the vagaries of fashion and the increasing prosperity among the new urban oligarchies that led them to erect such monuments. However, the fact that these kinds of tombs became increasingly common all over Europe in the wake of the fourteenth-century plagues is surely more than coincidental, and may at least in part have been a reaction to the ignominies of unceremonious, unmarked mass burials. In Flanders, for example, people chose ever more elaborate funerary sculpture – and the plague of 1400, which was particularly severe in Douai, led to the greatest demand for tombs with marble sculptures depicting the deceased with a spouse. Such tomb-styles were not new: double-effigy tombs had developed everywhere by the fourteenth century to represent the state of marriage. An example of this in Ireland is the double effigy tomb of William Goer and his wife, Margaret, in St Mary's Church in Kilkenny. From the mid-fifteenth century the Dublin/Meath school produced a number of these double effigies, which were decorated with human figures, saints and angels. Examples include the Purcell tomb in St Werburgh's in Dublin and that of Margaret Jenico and her husband in St Audoen's.[39] (See Plate 22)

Developing from these double-effigy tombs were the increasingly popular double-decker or transi tombs: on the top a representation of the deceased as he or she looked when alive and underneath a sculpture of the dead, worm-eaten corpse. Transi tombs capture the dichotomy between the dead in their full importance when alive and their representation as a corpse. No doubt, the ever-present threat of plague and almost certain death accounts much for the popularity of this new fashion in tomb sculpture: this was how people perceived the world. The transi tomb was seen as an appropriate image with which to comment on a life and death: life was vulnerable, fragile, short and death was the great leveller, mocker of human pretensions and agent of Fortune's Wheel. In the fifteenth century large funerary monuments became more popular and in particular cadaver tombs in which the deceased is portrayed as a corpse, with the emphasis on decay and finality. The eye sockets are empty, the body realistically become food for worms. This is evident in the tomb erected about 1482 for James Rice, a former mayor of Waterford city, and his wife, one of the best preserved of its kind. (See Plate 23) In the Rice tomb, the cadaverous figures are intended not to shock, but as a *memento mori*, to remind the viewer of his or her own mortality and of the need for repentance. The accompanying inscription, representative of the epitaphs usual on this type of tomb, expresses the hope that the prayers of the living will aid the dead in the journey beyond death:

> Here lie James Rice, onetime citizen of this city, founder of this chapel, and Catherine Broun, his wife. Whoever you may be, passerby, stop, weep as you read. I am what you are going to be, and I was what you are. I beg of you, pray for me! It is our lot to pass through the jaws of death. Lord Christ, we beg of thee, we implore thee, be merciful to us! Thou who has come to redeem the lost condemn not the redeemed![40]

The cadaver tomb is often cited as exemplifying what is perceived by some as the late medieval obsession with death and putrefaction. A typical example of this in Ireland is the Beaulieu cadaver tombstone, where the body has literally become food for worms, and the world of the spirit is very distant, if not absent. (see Plate 24) These late medieval Irish tombs then reveal an increased awareness of the sorrow of death and its terrors. In general this alteration, subtle as it is, does not become evident in Irish funerary sculpture until the fifteenth century, though this may also be merely a reflection of the fact that so few monuments survive from the 1350-1450 period.

A similar concern with suffering and death is evident in the metalwork that survives from this period. Some forty metal processional crosses and crucifixes survive from the late medieval period, some dating from the 1340s though most from the early and mid-fifteenth century. As elsewhere in Europe, the fourteenth-century crosses focus on the suffering of the crucified Christ and the figure is depicted twisted and in pain. Many see in this a reflection and expression of the concerns of a plague-stricken people. However, such perceptions gradually changed accordingly as plague came to be accepted as yet another disease in the medieval pantheon. As Dr Colm Hourihane in his study of these crosses writes, those of the fifteenth century begin to evince a change of focus:

> By the early fifteenth century the body lacks the distorted position of the previous century and has a stronger focus on realism and victory. Christ is shown in death with his arms upraised and his head resting on his shoulder. By the mid to late-fifteenth century the victory of Christ over death was being depicted. He is still shown with all the agony of the Crucifixion, ranging from the wound in the side to the hollow of the stomach and the exaggerated ribcage, but his head is more vertical and confident in posture.[41]

Negative evidence dominates what else remains of Irish art from the later fourteenth century. Very little visual art in general survives in Ireland from this time. This may partly have been due to the destruction of medieval monuments at later points in history, notably during the Reformation and the Cromwellian eras. However, the period 1350-1450 marks a hiatus in the production of funerary sculpture in Ireland generally. The most obvious cause of this disruption is the devastation of the Black Death on Dublin and other cities where most of the artistic activity was carried on. This disruption was evident elsewhere also. In Europe in general architectural projects already underway were abandoned during the Black Death and for many decades afterwards few new projects were undertaken. No major church building was undertaken after the Black Death until the sixteenth century when St Peter's in Rome was begun. In Ireland too, church building came to a halt, at least until the second half of the fifteenth century. This negative evidence speaks to a high rate of mortality among sculptors and masons in Ireland; in Europe at large this section of the population was badly hit by the plague outbreaks of 1348 and 1361, for reasons that cannot always be satisfactorily explained. Since most masons' and sculptors' workshops were in the cities and towns of Leinster most affected by the plague, their work was interrupted. This is particularly evident – ironically given the number who died in some of those towns – in the relative dearth of funerary sculpture. Whereas in England many tombs survive from this period, in Ireland there are only about nine funerary monuments extant for the period 1350-1450.[42]

Yet, continuation is the dominant theme of the artistic expression of these centuries. Church building did not stop completely and the skills of earlier eras were continued into the fifteenth century, even if they were simply continuations of earlier styles. However, there was a change. Thanks to the impact of plague, the cessation of immigration to Ireland and the increasingly warlike state of the country, contact with England, at least outside the Pale, lessened, and with it English influence on Irish architecture. Irish masons began to develop their own style (Irish Late-Gothic), ignoring the Perpendicular or the English Late-Gothic style of the fifteenth century. The architecture historian, Roger Stalley, sums up the change:

> About 1350 a stylistic watershed was reached following which the isolation of Irish architecture became more marked… It was an era of retrenchment that must have had a devastating impact on the masons' yards and it is hard to see how any continuity of training or apprenticeship could have survived.

In the following century, the new sculpture evinces more obvious Gaelic-Irish characteristics, reflecting the increasing domination of the Gaelic-Irish generally.[43]

While most of the new building took place, not in Dublin, but in the West under the patronage of the increasingly independent Gaelic-Irish lords and mendicant orders, some recovery was also evident in Dublin. Christ Church Cathedral was extended in the 1350s and St Patrick's Cathedral was renovated. Less is known about non-ecclesiastical building. Buildings, we know, fell into decay as the population of the city declined, but the extent of this cannot be ascertained. After the Black Death, though again not solely because of it, secular building patterns in Ireland changed, thanks to new demands and new fashions. From the late fourteenth century and continuing into the succeeding centuries, the large castles typical of the Anglo-Norman settlement were replaced by tower-houses, smaller stone, fortified houses that were obviously more economical both to build and defend. In 1429 Henry VI issued a statute promising a subsidy of £10 to any liege man in the Pale counties (Dublin, Louth, Meath and Kildare) who built a fortified castle or tower. Among the most famous of these 'ten pound castles' are two outside Dublin, Corr Castle in Howth, and the Dalkey tower house. Within the city boundaries, the trend towards building in stone continued, though this would take many centuries to complete.

We can say then that if there is an alteration in artistic consciousness in the post-plague era, it is more one of emphasis than of any radical change: death's more macabre details are foregrounded, its inevitability, universality and terror emphasised. Above all, the dearth of artistic evidence from this period speaks to the dislocation caused by the plague in the troubled conditions of late fourteenth-century Ireland.

CHAPTER FOUR

Long-Term Effects

The long-term significance of the Black Death is a subject of widely-varying judgements by historians. It has been viewed as the crucible of the modern world, marking 'a divide' in the history of medieval Europe and bringing about the end of the Middle Age, even 'a convulsion of the human race' and 'the greatest biological-environmental event in human history'.[1] While emphasising that its effects were to reinforce already existing trends, there is not any doubt that it had profound long-term consequences for those countries and cities it affected. The sudden mortality and the decline in population precipitated by the plague created disruption and labour shortages that had repercussions in all areas of life, administrative, economic and social. Similar trends are evident in Dublin. While in the short term the Black Death caused only a very temporary administrative dislocation in the city, in the long term it helped exacerbate the city's existing economic, social and political problems.

ADMINISTRATIVE DISRUPTION

Though there is little information regarding the short-term effects of the plague on the execution of day-to-day business in Dublin, and though the contemporary records might lead one to think the city's authorities attempted to carry on with business as usual, disruption there must have been. We do know that during later outbreaks of the plague in Dublin, the administration was temporarily suspended. This happened in 1382 when, 'on account of plague or pestilence', all parliamentary and judicial business was adjourned until mid-October. One hundred years and many outbreaks later, people were still so afraid of plague that in 1489 parliament in Dublin was prorogued because '…the fear of pestilence prevents the coming thither of lords, ecclesiastics and lawyers'. There are no such explicit references extant indicating any dislocation of parliamentary business in 1348-1350, but the absence of evidence in itself indicates a hiatus. Between 1341 and 1348, parliament sat five times: in November 1341, April 1345, June 1345, October 1346 and May 1348. The next parliament did not meet until 25 June 1350 and two sessions were then held in 1351, on 17 October and again on 31 October. Though parliamentary sessions were held irregularly in the period 1340-1350, nevertheless the complete gap between May 1348 and June 1350 suggests that the outbreak of the plague caused the suspension of parliament, as well as presumably of many other public functions. Throughout the whole decade 1340-1350 only five parliaments were convened, by comparison with nine in 1330-1340 and eleven in 1350-1360.[2]

The administration of justice experienced similar disruption. In the list of sessions of the Justiciar's court – that is, pleas held before the chief governor – for this period, the impact of the Black Death is intimated. In the year 1345, sixty-one sessions of the court were held; in 1346 this dropped to seventeen, without any sessions being recorded for the period April to September. In the following year, 112 sessions of the court were conducted, an unusually high number. Then in 1348 the number dropped again: no sessions are recorded for the period January to October 1348; eight were held in October 1348, the time when the Black Death was spreading throughout Dublin and surrounding areas; only two sessions were held in November and two in December. Disruption becomes most obvious in 1349, presumably when the impact of mortality and upheaval in the wake of the plague had made itself fully felt. Only two sessions are recorded for the whole year, on 12 January and 20 January. Nor are any sessions recorded for the year 1350. Business was resumed in January 1351 and sixty-seven sessions are recorded for that year, no doubt to catch up on the backlog caused by the break from January 1349 to January 1351.[3]

Moreover, of the sessions held in 1348 and 1349, none was held in Dublin or environs, but rather in the south of the country, in Tralee, County Kerry; Cork City; Buttevant, County Cork; and Kilmallock, County Limerick. All these towns, with the possible exception of Cork, were in areas where the plague would not yet have penetrated to any significant degree. When sessions resumed in 1351, they were held not only in Buttevant and Kilmallock, but also in those Leinster towns which had formerly featured prominently in the lists: Dublin as well as Naas, Kilkenny, Wexford, Trim, Drogheda, Carlow and Wexford. Contemporary documents do not offer an explanation for these gaps and changes of venue. However, that such disruptions should have taken place in the years when the plague was spreading throughout Dublin cannot be merely coincidental. The declining population also resulted in a decline in business for the Justiciar's court as suggested by an order on 25 March 1351 that there were to be only two justices in the future, as this was considered an adequate number to deal with the work of the Common Bench.[4]

LABOUR SHORTAGES: RESPONSES AND CONSEQUENCES

The higher mortality in the plague years had an immediate effect on the labour market. Thanks to the shortage of workers, wages in Dublin as elsewhere spiralled upwards and the economic conditions of survivors everywhere improved in the years immediately after the plague. As elsewhere in Europe and England, the initial response of the authorities was to protect the status quo and check inflation by freezing wage levels and prices and by re-imposing labour services. Attempts were also made to cap the price increases that followed on the labour shortage. In August 1349 the Justiciar ordered the mayor and bailiffs of Dublin 'to proclaim publicly at Dublin and cause the observance there of the provisions of the Statute of Labourers and Servants'. The Statute addressed the problem thus:

> Since a great part of the population, and especially workers
> and employees, has now died in this pestilence, many people,
> observing the needs of masters and the shortage of employ-
> ees, are refusing to work unless they are paid an excessive
> salary.

The Statute in dealing with non-agricultural labourers specifically addressed a wide-ranging array of artisans – saddlers,
skinners, white-tawers, cordwainers, tailors, smiths, carpenters,
masons, tilers, shipwrights, carters, butchers, fishmongers,
hostlers, brewers, bakers, pullers – all of whom by implication
were in a position to demand higher wages. An attempt was
made to freeze prices at their pre-plague levels, by issuing a
clear order to the vendors of victuals of all kinds. They were to
sell their products at reasonable prices, in line with the prices
being asked by their competitors, or else risk a penalty:

> The price should allow the seller a moderate, but not excessive,
> profit, taking reasonable account of the distance he has trans-
> ported the goods. And if a victualler should make a sale con-
> trary to the ordinance, and be convicted for it, then let him pay
> twice what he has received to the injured party, or, failing him,
> to the person who has been willing to bring the prosecution…

Every effort was made to marshal all possible sources of labour
and the 'sturdy beggar' became a particular focus of interest.
Surprisingly, neither the availability of work nor the increase in
wages seemed to hold any inducements for the many beggars
in the city who, according to the drafters of the Statute, preferred 'to beg in idleness rather than work for their living'. The
Statute directly addressed this problem:

And since many sturdy beggars – finding that they can make a living by begging for alms – are refusing to work, and are spending their time instead in idleness and depravity, and sometimes in robberies and other crimes; let no one presume, on pain of imprisonment, to give anything by way of charity or alms to those who are perfectly able to work, or to support them in their idleness, so that they will be forced to work for a living.[5]

However, the only solution to the problem was to issue ordinances and attempt to ensure compliance. The Statute of Labourers was read out in churches in order to ensure that the ordinances would be disseminated as widely as possible.

Beggars, especially 'sturdy' or able-bodied beggars, were the object of legislation in later medieval Dublin. They were seen as agents of plague dissemination, as well as 'wasters' at a time of labour shortage.

The problem of vagrants and beggars was not a new one. Alexander de Bicknor, Archbishop of Dublin from 1317 until his death in 1349, had already preached a sermon on the subject in Christ Church Cathedral. Though the text of the sermon has been lost, a seventeenth-century summary has survived listing the Archbishop's complaints:

> He bitterly complained of the mischiefs arising from the stragglers and beggars that infested the city and suburbs of Dublin and, so warm was he in his discourse, that he cursed every one that would not exercise some trade or calling every day, more or less. His sermon had such influence, that the then Mayor of Dublin exercised his authority upon the occasion, and would not suffer an idle person within his liberties, but such who spun or knit, as they walked the streets; even the begging Friars were not excused.[6]

This sermon echoes the problems presented by the multitudes of beggars and destitute who were fixtures in medieval cities throughout Europe, and particularly in the wake of the plague when many flocked into urban areas. Clearly they aroused resentments among the population at large and particularly so at times of labour shortage. The complaints were memorably expressed by Langland in his poem, *Piers the Ploughman*:

> And there were tramps and beggars hastening on their rounds, with their bellies and their packs crammed full of bread. They lived by their wits, and fought over their ale – for God knows, they go to bed glutted with food and drink, these brigands and get up with foul language and filthy talk; and all day long, Sleep and shabby Sloth are at their heels.

The plague severely aggravated the problem of beggars in England also, and repeated efforts were made to address it throughout the later decades of the century. An ordinance by Richard II in 1383 recognised that 'felters [idlers] and vagrants' overran the country 'more abundantly than they were heretofore accustomed.' Similar legislation was enacted against beggars and vagabonds in many European cities, with the intention of mobilizing all possible sources of labour.[7]

The ordinances of the Statute of Labourers were repeated many times in subsequent years. They were reissued for the whole country by the Great Council in Kilkenny in 1351. This met with little success, as in 1366, the Statutes of Kilkenny had to regulate once more the wages of carpenters, plasterers, tilers, potters and apprentices and attempted to freeze wages by threatening judicial sanctions on any labourer who refused to accept a 'reasonable maintenance'. Clearly, the plague had the effect of strengthening the economic clout of workers who were now in a bargaining position.[8]

The labour shortage also had immediate effects on the administration of the Church and the task of filling the depleted ecclesiastical ranks became pressing. The problem of ensuring a literate, educated clergy had already been a major concern of the hierarchy in pre-plague Ireland and the papal registers are strewn with references to the lack of able and qualified candidates. A university in Dublin had been planned in 1321 to remedy the situation, but nothing came of it. After the Black Death and subsequent outbreaks, the pool of educated clergy shrank even further. There does not seem to have been any shortage of candidates, but many of these were illiterate, in the medieval sense of not knowing Latin, or were in some other way unsuitable for office. In the post-plague years the ecclesiastical authorities were forced to bend the traditional requirements for entry to the priesthood. Knighton's account of events in England is perhaps typical of what happened in many places:

> At that time there was such a great shortage of priests everywhere that many churches were widowed and lacked the divine offices, Masses, matins, vespers, and the sacraments and sacramentals. A man could scarcely get a chaplain for less than £10 or 10 marks to minister to any church, and whereas before the pestilence there had been a glut of priests, and a man could get a chaplain for 4 or 5 marks, or for 3 marks with board and lodging, in this time there was scarcely anyone who would accept a vicarage at £20 or 20 marks. But within a short time a great crowd of men whose wives had died in the pestilence rushed into priestly orders. Many of them were illiterate, no better than laymen – for even if they could read, they did not understand what they read.[9]

In France, the contemporary chronicler Jean de Venette attributed the ignorance that flourished in the wake of the Black Death to the fact that '...few men could be found in houses, towns or castles who were able or willing to instruct boys in the rudiments of Latin'. In Ireland also many 'illiterate' candidates were appointed, much to the dismay of Archbishop FitzRalph of Armagh who considered the ignorance of the clergy to be so serious that in the first sermon he preached after the plague, in March 1349, he put it on a par with the pestilence as a reason to pray for the intercession of Mary. In November 1363 a group of clerks, some from Dublin, others from the neighbouring diocese of Meath and further afield petitioned the Pope for prebends in Ireland where 'by reason of pestilence and wars... there is a great lack of clerks, and the value of benefices is small'. They included a warning to the Pope that 'he must not be surprised that the persons have no scholastic degrees, inasmuch as in all Ireland there is no university or place of study'.[10]

In Ireland, as in England and the rest of Europe, the shortage of priests and of qualified candidates was so acute that the Church was also forced to relax its rules regarding the age and parentage of priests. Canon law forbade ordination to the priesthood to those under the age of twenty-four and to illegitimate candidates, defined as the offspring of clergy or of parents who had not been married in accordance with canon law. This requirement was gradually relaxed throughout Europe from the mid-fourteenth century and dispensations for underage and illegitimate candidates were increasingly sought and granted. Admittedly, one of the reasons for this increase was that the Avignon Papacy deliberately attempted to raise revenue by requesting a fee for dispensations. Still, this policy was also a response to demand and clearly there was a shortage of priests that had to be met in some way. Requirements were being relaxed in Ireland from the late 1330s and early 1340s, but the number of instances increased after 1348. In January 1349 the Archbishop of Dublin was given permission to ordain thirty illegitimate persons and twenty underage candidates to the priesthood. A separate order in the same year allowed him to ordain ten persons of his diocese, despite illegitimacy of any kind. And in 1363 he was granted blanket permission to ordain illegitimate candidates in general to the priesthood.[11]

Abbeys and friaries in the city faced a similar shortfall in the number of qualified candidates and had to make similar compromises in order to gain new recruits. The Franciscans everywhere grappled with inadequate numbers of new entrants and tried to resolve the problem by attracting very young candidates. The statutory age to enter the priesthood was lowered to fourteen, but the Franciscans in Ireland supposedly recruited candidates even under the age of thirteen, or at least so Archbishop FitzRalph of Armagh, no friend of the Franciscans, alleged. That some novices were attracted to the better living conditions offered in religious houses is indirectly suggested by a Papal decree of October 1348 granting leave to the Friars Preachers of England in Ireland:

> to eat flesh-meat on lawful days when they go out to preach the word of God…, the disturbances and consequent lack of food in Ireland making it impossible for friars to obtain the prescribed kinds of meat outside their houses, which causes a diminution of the persons entering the said order.[12]

However, the shortage of labour had further, more wide-ranging repercussions in both the secular and ecclesiastical spheres. The lack of suitable candidates for ecclesiastical office, together with the declining value of benefices, encouraged the practice of office-holders holding multiple benefices at one time. The *Calendar of Papal Petitions* noted that 'on account of the slender value of benefices and the scarcity of fit persons, it is hardly possible to subsist on two benefices'. Again, this was not a new phenomenon and was well established in Ireland by the early fourteenth century. However, it seems to have become even more widespread in the latter half of the century, particularly in the Leinster area where the wealthier benefices were held by ambitious ecclesiastics living elsewhere, usually in England. This practice required special permission and many of the requests for permission specifically mention the plague as one of the necessitating causes. In April 1351 Dublin's Archbishop John of St Paul was given Papal permission, to hold three or more benefices to the amount of 100 marks because of 'his income having suffered by the invasion of the enemies and the mortality in those parts'. The practice was nonetheless not officially condoned and efforts were made to put an end to it. In 1364 the Pope ordered the bishops of Ireland to report on all the benefices in Papal hands 'so that a stop may be put to pluralities and other scandals'. Charges were levied on non-resident officeholders, and the money collected was intended to pay for replacements. But these efforts met with little success. In 1378-1384 a group of twelve canons attached to St Patrick's Cathedral in Dublin but resident in England complained of the exorbitant charges being levied on non-resident officeholders. The practice was exemplified by Walter de Gnoushale, a canon of Dublin and treasurer of Leighlin. He was given permission to hold three benefices, despite being illegitimate; this licence was extended in April 1351 and in July 1351 was extended further to permission to hold any number of 'compatible' benefices. John Swayne, later Archbishop of Armagh, is another instance: in 1404 he was rector of Galtrim in Meath, treasurer of Dublin Cathedral, canon and prebendary of Newcastle Lyons, Dublin and of Taghmon in Ferns.[13]

The increasing incidence of pluralism also meant an intensification of the problem of absenteeism, as senior ecclesiastics, like their secular counterparts, increasingly left to take up offices and benefices in England, therby helping to erode further the extent of English influence in Ireland. This seems to have been particularly true of the Dublin area. A typical case was John de Briane who in August 1350 was given the canonry, prebend and deanery of St Patrick's Cathedral, Dublin, even though he already had cure of two churches and prebends in Exeter, Lichfield, Westbury, Worcester and Wolverhampton. The following year, in June 1351, he was allowed to keep the income from his benefices for five years, despite being non-resident while studying civil law at university. At the same time, the treasurer of the cathedral, John Gate, was given similar permission for three years. Efforts were made to limit the practice and in the later decades of the century there are numerous records of men being deprived of office because of absence. John Gedeney was deprived of the prebend of Tassagard in 1391; in 1432 the Archbishop of Dublin divided the revenue of the prebend of Swords in order to lessen the income of the absentee holders of the benefice; and in 1468 an Act of Parliament was passed decreeing that the income of the absentee canons in St Patrick's Cathedral was to be distributed among the resident canons.[14]

In the secular sphere, the government and administration of the city also were faced with the difficulties of finding suitable candidates able and willing to assume public office. In this case, the shortage had both demographic and social causes. Already in the earlier fourteenth century, there is evidence of people avoiding the elections for mayor and officers in Dublin. In 1306, for example, fines were imposed on eligible candidates who absented themselves from elections. This decree was repeated in 1316 when the citizens of Dublin made a list of requests concerning the stricter collection and supervision of debts, profits, taxes, rents and customs, the punishment of those who evaded their taxes and especially of those who did not attend the municipal elections which all citizens were required to attend.[15] The problem worsened as the century progressed. It became increasingly difficult in particular to persuade men to take up the office of Justiciar in Ireland. Richard of Pembridge in 1371 'utterly refused' to take up the office and in 1374 William of Windsor accepted it only under pressure.[16] By the mid-fifteenth century, as Dr G. Mac Niocaill has shown, the shortage of candidates in Dublin had become a pressing problem and the fact that with each new ordinance the fines were even more precisely stipulated indicates that solutions were not easily found. An ordinance of 1483 decreed that anybody elected to the office of bailiff who declined to take it up ran the risk of a £10 fine and of being deprived of his rights as a freeman. In 1485 any eligible candidate who absented himself from the assembly when the mayor was chosen was to be fined 40 shillings. Some citizens may even have bought immunity, or sub-contracted the duties of office, as did some wealthy men in Kilkenny. Dublin continued to experience difficulties in recruiting candidates right into the early sixteenth century, despite all the inducements that accompanied public office.

This contraction in the sense of civic responsibility was of course not peculiar to Dublin. Bristol and Coventry were among the English cities forced to contend with similar problems in the fifteenth century as leading citizens proved increasingly unwilling to assume public office. Furthermore, in many large cities in the post-plague era there is evidence not only of a decline in civic responsibility but also of an increasing defensiveness and self-interest in people's outlooks:

The Mayor of Dublin, after a 1384 representation.

Economic contraction was met by contraction of outlook; there was more concentration on the immediate locality, more jealousy of neighbouring towns, and often this was matched by a corresponding change in the type of man who made town policy.

Guilds become exclusionary, oligarchies came to dominate urban government, and in northwestern Europe towns vied with one another. Local industries were protected and promoted at the expense of those of neighbouring towns, as happened in Ghent for example. In this light the fact that Dublin-made pottery becomes more common in this period may be as much a testimony to protectionist policies as to any lessening of trade with the Continent. Just as Continental cities became more restrictive in the freedoms they allowed to outside industries and foreigners, so too in Dublin. In 1454 the mayor and bailiffs decreed that all those of Irish blood were to quit the city and many went to live in Irishtown. The decree was repeated in 1457 when the 'mere' Irish were again banished.

However, the reason for this contraction in Dublin civic life was not only one of declining morale and civic spirit. Population factors played a major role. Since only the wealthy could afford to take on the risks of public office, and since the numbers of wealthy were declining, there was a shrinking pool of candidates for administrative office. This can only be explained by a high death rate, which was no doubt aggravated by continuing outbreaks of plague, a low birth rate, which was most likely conditioned by the tendency of later outbreaks of plague to affect children and young people, and continuing emigration from the city. Mac Niocaill summ-arizes the position of the typical late medieval Irish town thus:

> Towards the end of the middle ages, the Irish town was suf-fering from a population crisis, not necessarily in the form of falling population at this period, but perhaps stagnation after a fall at an earlier period, which rendered difficult the recruit-ment of a governing class within the town; ... this difficulty was compounded by the concentration of wealth in the hands of a relative few within the towns, thus reducing the number of those who were in a position to answer for the faithful dis-charge of their duties ... [17]

Though the plague, at least in the short term, helped improve the lot of the labourer, all the available evidence from cities elsewhere in Europe would seem to suggest that the urban wealthy profited even more from the disruption of the period. The wealthy in their stone houses had more of a chance of escaping the plague, and had the reserves necessary to profit from the disruption of the post-plague era. The production of luxury goods, such as cloths, pewter and bronze increased as wealth became increasingly concentrated in the hands of the few. Everywhere, the gap between rich and poor widened significantly in the post-plague era. Just as in rural areas free peasants with large holdings were able to enlarge their holdings even further after the plague, so too in the cities a sim-ilar adjustment took place as the more established craftsmen and tradesmen acquired property and office. At the other end of the social scale, the poor became even poorer, just as rural cottiers drifted into becoming landless labourers or migrated to the city. In French cities and towns, for example, the incidence of prostitution increased, as did violence and drunkenness. Above all, the numbers of vagabonds and beggars increased and one English historian has even argued that it was the plague that brought the phenomenon of 'the sturdy beggar' to the fore.[18]

In cities elsewhere, high mortality, the redistribution of wealth, higher taxes, the enactment of restrictive labour laws, and the closing of ranks by urban oligarchies, all led to violent uprisings. Oftentimes the post-plague unrest and upris-ings were led by the guilds – such as in Nuremberg in 1348, Cologne in 1364, 1370 and 1396, Frankfurt in 1355, 1364-1365, Augsburg in 1370 and Florence in 1378. We do not have any record of any such disturbances in Dublin, perhaps because external threats by the Gaelic-Irish distracted attention from internal economic woes? Or perhaps with the exodus of workers from Dublin for English cities, the city avoided the resentments that developed elsewhere to the restrictive legislation of late fourteenth-century labour and sumptuary laws. Whatever the reason, there are no records of the kind of labour unrest that is recorded elsewhere. However, the level of violence was high. In September 1357, a Papal letter to the Archbishop of Dublin refers to:

> ...clerks and laymen who in that distant part of the world, where wars are almost continually being waged, [who] have incurred excommunication by taking part in the destruction of churches, towns and other places, burnings, slayings of ecclesiastics, and public spoliations.

In 1407, there were fears that even Dublin Castle would be taken 'by deceit of untrue men, strangers, and others dwelling in the marches of Ireland, who flock thither and enter the castle'. Two years later, in 1409, there is a report of people keeping 'kernes, coynes, hobelers, and idlemen', or basically private armies, within the county of Dublin. The presence of these private armies not only heightened the violence but, given the contemporary practice of coyne and livery - that is of quartering these troops and their horses on the local population - also would have entailed considerable hardship for the inhabitants of Dublin's suburbs. We do know of riots in Dublin due to poverty in 1512, which ended with the mayor being sentenced to walk through the city streets barefoot as punishment for not dealing with the riots quickly enough. But the 1350s have left no such record.[19]

DECLINING POPULATION AND ECONOMIC CONSEQUENCES

The Black Death has been credited with introducing radical changes in the economy of medieval Europe, and many would agree with the historian N.G. Pounds who concluded that it brought about an 'abrupt reversal' in economic development.[20] The Black Death did not so much bring about a reversal in Dublin's fortunes, but rather ensured that the city's already struggling economy would continue to weaken and that any hints at recovery would be blighted. The long-lasting economic effects of the plague's mortality are undoubted, evident in the many references to the food shortages, financial difficulties and tax arrears experienced in the later fourteenth century. After 1348, all the major towns in the colony were forced to petition for assistance because of their impoverishment and Dublin was no exception.

The impoverishment was not of course a recent phenomenon and had already been evident long before 1348. The rapid growth of the earlier Middle Ages had stopped by the beginning of the fourteenth century, thanks to war, famine and a host of other factors. Even before 1315, warfare had caused a contraction in the outlying areas and even within the city itself. A few instances indicate the extent of this. An inquisition of 1305 revealed that a tenement near the Abbey of St Thomas had not yielded any income to the city 'because no one dwelt there nor brewed ale for sale'. In 1326, burgages, houses and tenements lay waste in New Street and Patrick's Street and tenants were reported to be paying lower rents than formerly. In south County Dublin, on the manors of Castlekevin, Clondalkin, Rathcoole and Ballymore, holdings and townlands were said to be unoccupied or in Irish hands, and on the Archbishop of Dublin's manor of Tallaght only four betaghs remained and three townlands were alleged to be uninhabitable. On the royal demesne at Newcastle Lyons, the tenants were so poverty-stricken by the plundering and burning of the Bruces and their allies that they could no longer pay the farm they owed.[21] Then there were the many other factors peculiar to Ireland such as landlord absenteeism and the emigration of artisans and labourers. The result was the under-population of outlying rural settlements and a contraction within the city itself, a common phenomenon in contemporary Europe. However, whereas economic crises elsewhere led rural dwellers to move to larger towns and manors, in Ireland the cause was most often war or the fear of war. The persistence of warfare forced settlers, particularly in the more exposed march areas, to retreat further and further, leaving their lands tenantless. So in the marcher lands around Dublin we read of:

> certain persons holding lands both in the Irish marches and in peaceful places [who] flee to live in the latter, leaving the former waste and undefended and to the detriment of their English inhabitants.[22]

The fact then that the economy was already declining and vulnerable meant that the effects of the Black Death were felt all the more keenly, and that Dublin's economy offered few resources to enable its citizens to recover quickly from the plague's devastation.

The decline in population had immediate repercussions for the survivors, as the tax base was no longer adequate to support the city's expenses. With fewer citizens to contribute to the fee-farm or to the costs of maintaining the walls, the city fell into arrears in its tax payments, and was repeatedly forced to petition for tax relief and for grants to rebuild walls and bridges. A request for aid in 1351 specifically cited the citizens' impoverishment due to the pestilence:

> The merchants and other dwellers in the city are so impoverished as well by the late pestilence in their land as by other misfortunes that they require relief from other quarters to buy 1,000 quarters of wheat in England and trade with the same in Ireland.

Numerous grants and remissions of rent were granted to the city of Dublin in the second half of the fourteenth and the early fifteenth centuries. Its rent was remitted in 1355-1356; in 1363 a grant was made to enable the citizens 'to carry on their commerce'; again in 1423 rent remission was granted, 'in consideration of the great burthens sustained by the mayor, bailiffs and commonalty of Dublin, both in war and peace'. Similar difficulties were felt in the rural areas around Dublin. In the royal demesnes in Co. Dublin, for example, tenants complained they were entirely impoverished by the late pestilence and by the prises of the King's ministers.[23]

A decline is evident also in the financial health of the ecclesiastical authorities. Again, as in the secular sphere, this had already been damaged principally by the endemic warfare in the country from the early fourteenth century onwards as ecclesiastical institutions were forced to spend their revenues on defence and reconstruction. This drain on resources worsened through the fourteenth century as attacks on church property became more frequent. In the Diocese of Dublin alone, poverty was not an uncommon complaint by many abbeys and benefices in the early fourteenth century, and this despite their vast holdings. St Mary's Abbey in Dublin alone held 17,125 acres in Co. Dublin in the Middle Ages out of a total area of 222,710 acres, while the Archbishop of Dublin held about 53,200 acres. Yet St Mary's Abbey, as well as the Hospital of St John the Baptist outside Newgate, the Hospital of St John of Jerusalem, and others, all pleaded poverty at this time because of attacks by the Irish. The Hospital of St John the Baptist was forced to remit the arrears of rent on some of its properties in Dublin and reduced the rents in the 1330s and 1340s.[24] A similar situation existed among the secular clergy: in August 1307 the Archbishop-elect of Dublin was permitted to retain all his benefices, 'the debts of the see being heavy on account of its frequent violence and the wars in which it has suffered'. In the 1302-1306 papal taxation list many outlying churches on the borders of the diocese were returned as waste due to war. Escalating taxation to fund local defence needs as well as the King's wars in France further exacerbated the decline in revenue.[25]

This decline gained momentum after the plague and, in contemporary accounts, war and pestilence are mentioned together as its inseparable agents. In 1353, the income of the Archbishop of Dublin was reported to have been severely affected both by the mortality caused by the plague as well as by the attacks of the Irish. In 1390 the Priory of Holy Trinity at Christ Church was reported to be so 'impoverished by war and pestilence' that its diocesan taxes were reduced by half and by a further half in 1426. The Augustinian Priory of All Hallows was likewise granted a reduction in its diocesan taxes in 1421. By 1410, the Priory of Kilmainham was so stricken 'by mortality and other disasters' that its revenues were not sufficient for defence. In St Patrick's Cathedral, the Dean and Chapter were exempted from paying taxes because 'their possessions are much diminished'. Special indulgences were granted in 1400 to those who gave alms to the church and the hospital in the Priory of St John the Baptist. In the same year, the fortunes of the Abbey of St Thomas the Martyr were reported to have so dwindled that it could sustain only sixteen canons where formerly there had been thirty-six; the churches on which it relied for support had been depopulated 'through hostile incursions, rapines, fires and slayings of the parishioners, pestilences and other misfortunes'.[26]

The fortunes of the Priory and Hospital of St John the Baptist at Newgate in the later medieval period mirror those of many other abbeys in the city at this time. Dr Mark Hennessy in his study of the priory has shown how, from the 1320s, its revenues from lands both in the Dublin area as well as elsewhere in Ireland were severely affected by warfare. In 1334 the monks complained that their possessions were 'greatly wasted by the hostile attacks of Scots and Irish' and this decline continued for the next hundred years and more. A similar decline is evident in its revenue from its urban properties. Throughout the 1330s and 1340s it was forced to remit the rent arrears on some of its Dublin properties and even in some instances reduce the rent because of the financial difficulties of the tenants. The advent of the Black Death served to consolidate this decline. By 1400 the priory could no longer adequately cater for the poor in its care or for the upkeep of the church. This downward trend was to continue into the fifteenth century and later. By the time of the dissolution of the monasteries in 1539 only fifty beds were available in its hospital.[27]

One is left to deduce the effects of this shortage of funds and manpower, not only on the labour market, but also on the upkeep of the city's buildings, churches and institutions. Contemporary urban records elsewhere create a picture of cities where houses and churches fell into decay, plots were left uncultivated and whole areas abandoned. Neglected and crumbling buildings would have posed a severe hazard in the narrow streets of a medieval town. Knighton writes that in England after the plague, '…many buildings, both large and small, in all the cities, boroughs and townships decayed and were utterly razed to the ground for want of occupants'. In Cork numerous houses were left empty after the plague and by 1351 were reported to be falling into ruin. In Dublin gaps in the archaeological record for this time indicate severe disruption in the commercial life of the city. In excavations in Patrick Street, researchers discovered an absence of stratified deposits from the later part of the fourteenth and into the fifteenth centuries, negative evidence of the plague's devastation, though investigators acknowledged that there could have been other causes for this also.[28] Many churches fell into disrepair and authorities were forced to adopt measures to help pay for their restoration. The Church of St Peter de Hulle, outside the city, was 'by deaths and pestilences …brought to ruin' and in May 1371 an indulgence was granted to penitents who gave alms for the restoration of the church. In 1394, a similar indulgence was promised to those who gave alms for the repair of St Patrick's Cathedral whose bell-tower had fallen, damaging a large section of the church. Other religious houses had to cut back their services, presumably due to declining numbers and resources. At a time when one might expect existing hospitals to have been overrun with patients, a record of 1373 from the Hospital of St John without Newgate indicates that the monastery could sustain only 115 infirm paupers besides its chaplain and lay brothers, by contrast with the 155 persons it had cared for at the beginning of the century.[29]

Nor did the city quickly recover. With a declining tax base and an ever-shrinking population in the wake of the plague and its later outbreaks, the surviving citizens were even more burdened by the mounting taxes necessary for the upkeep of the city's fabric. As late as 1427 the mayor, bailiffs and commons of Dublin were complaining that many had left, with the result that the city suffered 'manifest desolation' and its walls, forts and towers had become 'weak and ruinous'.[30]

The plague's devastation of the rural population in the surrounding villages of Co. Dublin also had repercussions for the city. Manors along the marches, particularly to the south-east, which were already under economic strain, were hard hit by the plague. The food supply to the city was thereby disrupted, as were the city's defences, as the manors could no longer act as buffers against the marauding attacks of the Gaelic-Irish. This happened on the archiepiscopal manors at Finglas, Swords, Tallaght and Clondalkin. In 1354, the demesne tenants and farmers of the King's demesnes in County Dublin petitioned for royal help, pleading total impoverishment due to the 'late pestilence' and 'excessive prises' of the King's ministers in Ireland. Tenant shortages continued to be felt into the 1360s on these royal manors in Dublin and reached such a pitch that, in 1362, orders were issued to lease vacant lands to all willing takers. Nor was there any respite: vacant holdings are still being reported for the royal demesnes of Crumlin, Saggard and Newcastle Lyons into the 1360s.[31]

Not surprisingly then, the combination of the labour shortages in the city as well as in surrounding rural areas, together with the general disruption in the manorial economy intensified problems with the food supply in the city. Dublin's difficulties were further compounded by the fact that lands to the south were so often attacked by the Gaelic-Irish. In the years after the plague, Dublin was forced to procure corn in Wales, England and even France for the maintenance of its citizens. In 1352, license was granted to the civic authorities to buy wheat in England and trade with it in Ireland because they were 'so impoverished as well by the late pestilence in their land as by other misfortunes'. A general prohibition on the export of corn was imposed, though exemptions were granted in 1352, 1353 and subsequently. In 1364, prices had risen so high that the citizens were again complaining they were being destroyed and impoverished, and were suffering immense hardship. By 1394 the food supply was under such threat that the export of provisions from all corporate towns in Ireland was forbidden. An uncertain food supply posed severe hardship for the citizens of Dublin. At the end of the century, in 1399, Jean Creton, a French visitor with Richard ɪɪ's second expedition, commented on the food shortages in Dublin where he saw four to six soldiers having to share a loaf of bread, some going hungry for five days, and concluded that:

I should have been heartily glad to have been penniless in Poitiers or Paris, because here [in Dublin] there was no amusement or mirth, only trouble, toil and danger.

The problems in the food supply were somewhat alleviated when licenses were granted to those living in border areas to trade with the Gaelic-Irish. However, difficulties continued into the next century and by 1437 grain, and later corn and beans, were being exported to Ireland from Bristol. In the 1450s concern about the food supply again became particularly pressing and many ordinances were passed forbidding the export of corn to England and Wales. Clearly, this created great difficulties for the citizens, and had serious ramifications for the city's trade.[32]

Dublin's trade, as elsewhere in Ireland, was already declining even before the advent of the Black Death. The city suffered from numerous threats, both natural and military: its port continued to silt up, making it unsuitable for the delivery and unloading of cargo; its communication with the hinterland was threatened by the inroads of the Gaelic-Irish in Wicklow. Then the population decrease in the wake of the Black Death led to lower demand for basic agricultural products as well as other products. This, together with a multiplicity of other factors, both external and internal, affected the volume of trade in general, which declined even further in the fifteenth century. For example, Dublin imported approximately 1,260 tuns of wine in 1301-1303; by 1346-1366 this had dropped to 180 tuns a year. A similar decline was evident in other products.

The customs returns for Dublin indicate, though do not prove, a general decline in the volume of trade from the 1320s onwards. Some recovery was evident in the early 1340s, but the lowest point was reached in 1345-1351. The following are average yearly returns for these years.

AVERAGE YEARLY CUSTOMS RETURNS

IN DUBLIN 1311–1351

1311–1312	£146	2s	0d
1320–1322	£79	19s	4d
1323–1325	£80	14s	0d
1341–1342	£67	13s	1d
1342–1345	£82	4s	0d
1345–1351	£52	6s	7d

Customs returns continued to decline and in 1369 the returns amounted only to £59 8s 1d.[33]

By the end of the fifteenth century the export of grain and cereals from Dublin had come to an end. New exports and imports were coming to the fore such as hides, cloth, wine and fish. These were exported principally to Flanders and Italy as well as England and in this trade Dublin did not prosper as much as other ports. This is a reflection of developments all over Europe: cities such as Lincoln, Winchester, Florence and Bruges all declined in the fourteenth century and others such as Venice, Antwerp, Amsterdam, Coventry and Bristol came to the fore.[34] This type of regional redistribution was also evident in Ireland and in the fifteenth century ports on the southern and western coasts, such as Youghal, Galway, Limerick, Sligo and Dingle, all experienced increasing prosperity. The reasons for this shift are complex. The decline and obvious financial difficulties of eastern ports such as Dublin undoubtedly played a part and in this the Black Death was instrumental. The fact that the plague affected the Leinster area more severely than the Gaelic sector is of considerable significance in view of the changing balance of power, whether political or economic. A certain redistribution of wealth took place in the post-plague era, away from the colony to Gaelic areas, evident in the thriving trade of its harbours on the western and southwestern coasts and in the literary and architectural revival in Gaelic areas. By contrast, the colony's economy continued to contract, mirroring its political and military contraction.

LABOUR MOBILITY: IMMIGRATION AND EMIGRATION

Elsewhere in the cities of Europe, the post-plague labour shortage was gradually overcome as rural workers migrated from plague-stricken rural areas to the cities. This phenomenon of the movement of labour was a common one on the Continent and in England in the wake of the plague of 1348, as labourers and smaller tenants moved in search of higher wages and the opportunities created by the labour shortage in the towns. Some urban authorities in Italy, such as in Siena and Venice for example, offered the inducements of citizenship and freedom from taxes to all those who would come to exercise a trade in their cities. Thus, the populations of Continental cities in the wake of the plague were continually augmented or at least stabilized by immigration, with immigrants from the countryside constituting an estimated one third of the population at any given time.[35] Some of the larger towns in Ireland may also have benefited, in the short term, from agricultural labourers moving to the city. There is some evidence that Gaelic-Irish migrated to the towns also at this time. A record of August 1360 refers to the 'great numbers of mere Irish [who] are admitted to dwell in divers [sic] cities, boroughs and towns of Ireland'. This migration was limited however, and was not welcomed by the city's authorities. In 1359, an ordinance was passed decreeing that 'no mere Irishman of Irish race shall be made mayor, bailiff, janitor or other officer or minister'. This was followed some decades later by a ban on the employment of Gaelic-Irish apprentices within the city.[36] Irish towns, in general, were not replenished with rural immigrants. Rather, they experienced net emigration and therefore continued to manifest the same shortage of labourers that was evident in the countryside. Nor were there any more immigrants from England whose population was already declining due to the effects of plague. This stagnation in the urban population in Ireland is in contrast to England where continuing immigration from the countryside offset the worst effects of plague depopulation in the towns and allowed for the expansion of cities such as Norwich and Coventry.

In general, in England and Ireland, the mobility of labour was regarded with suspicion and the authorities attempted to contain it with repressive measures. In England, ordinances were passed forbidding labourers and employees from leaving their place of employment without official letters of permission or letters patent. The problem was even more pressing in Ireland as people left the country altogether for England where conditions were considerably more favourable. The Statutes of Kilkenny in 1366 attempted to halt the exodus from towns and countryside:

> Since the common labourers are for the greatest part absent, and fly out of the said land; it is agreed and assented, that, because living and victuals are dearer than they were wont to be, each labourer in his degree, according to the discretion of two of the

most substantial and discreet men of the city, town, borough, village, or hamlet, in the country where he shall perform his labour, shall receive his maintenance reasonably, in gross or by the day, and if they will not do so, nor be obedient, they shall be taken before the mayor, seneschal, sovereign, provost or bailiff of the cities or towns where they are, or by the sheriff of the county, and put in prison, until the coming of the justices assigned who will come twice in the year into every county and the justice of the chief place, who shall award due punishment for the same, and right to the parties who shall feel themselves aggrieved thereby. And that no labourer shall pass beyond sea; and in case that he shall do so and shall return, he shall be taken and put in prison for a year and afterwards make fine at the King's will.[37]

Again, in 1388 the Statute of Labourers was further amended to include even stricter controls on the movement of labour. All employees and labourers were required to carry letters patent stating where they were going and when they would return whenever they left their place of employment; any employee or labourer found contravening this would be put in the stocks which were maintained in every town for that purpose. Similar requirements were imposed on pilgrims, wandering scholars and religious. Fixed wage rates were laid down for the different classes of labourer. Able-bodied men and women were forbidden to beg, and those unfit to work had to remain within their own jurisdictions. Such repressive legislation continued to be enacted into the fifteenth century to deal with the continuing shortage of rural labourers – a man with less than 20 shillings a year in land was debarred from apprenticing his sons to a craft, for example. This type of legislation, where enacted, had the effect of further aggravating the shortage of labour in the cities.[38]

Emigration from Dublin to England became an increasingly serious problem. This was not of course a purely post-plague phenomenon, and had been a cause of concern from the beginning of the thirteenth century. However, it became widespread and persistent as the fourteenth century drew to a close. People left for cities such as Bristol, where for a few decades many prospered, eventually becoming mayors and successful tradesmen. In an attempt to stem the flow, measures had already been passed in the 1340s requiring licences to emigrate. While definite figures are not available, the increasing number of references in contemporary documents to the problem after 1348 would seem to suggest that the plague helped intensify the process, and continuing emigration in turn aggravated the population loss already occasioned by the plague. Initially, legislation dealt mainly with officeholders. In 1353 all officeholders as well as landowners were forbidden to leave Ireland on pain of forfeiting their possessions. These measures were repeated in 1359 and 1361. Measures were also enacted to deal with the flight of labourers and artisans. Official permission to emigrate was made an even more stringent requirement. In 1391-1399, official permission to emigrate was granted to 521 clerks, craftsmen, labourers and artisans; however, this figure very likely does not reflect the actual numbers who left Ireland at this time, as there were undoubtedly many others who left the country unofficially. When the licensing requirement proved ineffective, other measures were passed, attempting to penalize those who transported unlicensed persons. Clearly, these injunctions were not effective either as they were repeated in 1410, 1412, 1415 and again in 1421. By 1421, according to a contemporary report, every day saw 'great numbers' of labourers and artisans leaving Ireland for England where they stayed.[39]

Evidence from England indicates that people left from Ireland in such significant numbers that they generated considerable hostility among the English. Irish merchants travelling from Chester to Coventry, Oxford and London were frequently attacked. That the influx from Ireland was considerable is further underlined by the many restrictive measures adopted by cities in England. Bristol, for example, was particularly affected by the flow of migrants from Dublin and in 1439 forbade the admission of any Irish-born person to the city council. The numbers of Irish students allowed entry to Oxford and Cambridge was restricted, and the London Inns of Court banned Irish students. Ironically, these people, who were considered 'liege' men while living in Dublin or other Irish towns, once in England were classified as alien and were subject to taxes imposed on aliens for the right to live in England. In 1440 a poll-tax was imposed on all aliens residing in England, and the Anglo-Irish were included in the category of 'aliens'. This aroused such opposition that, two years later, this categorisation was dropped and they were no longer classified as aliens. Such measures reflect measures adopted in cities all over Europe: retraction was the immediate and most common response to the worsening economic situation. Partly as a response to the exodus from Ireland that had left so many towns under-populated and vulnerable, schemes were introduced to repatriate Irish living in England. In 1394 all Irish-born men living in England were ordered to return home, and while over 500 were exempted from the order, many more must have returned rather than face the severe fines that would have otherwise been imposed. Yet others were able to purchase exemptions from the King. Still, the success of the order is somewhat in doubt given that similar orders were repeated in

1413 when a decree was passed ordering all the 'wylde' Irish, except those who held honourable positions, to leave England.[40]

The flow of people out of the towns continued and over the next fifty-odd years, towns all over the colony in their petitions for aid made specific reference to the difficulties caused by this exodus. The combination of continuing mortality, low replacement rates and high emigration meant an ever-decreasing tax base and an ever-heavier burden on the remaining citizens. The precise role that plague and pestilence played in this is impossible to measure. But contemporaries frequently name it as one of the causes of their misfortunes. In 1427, the mayor, bailiffs and commons of Dublin in their petition for aid specifically put the plague first in their list of reasons why people were fleeing the city:

> Owing to pestilence, incursions and divers [sic] heavy burthens in the time of the King and his progenitors, the citizens were unable to pay the rent to the Crown without imposing tallage on the commonalty. Many of the commons had subsequently left Dublin and would not return to the city, on which great loss and manifest desolation was thus entailed.

In 1435 the authorities of numerous other towns and cities complained that they were 'on the point to be famished' because 'the few liege people left were not sufficient to victual' the cities. Whereas populations elsewhere tended to rebound quickly, clearly this did not happen in Dublin, thanks to the endless circle of continual war, recurring plague and emigration.[41]

DUBLIN: A COLONIAL OUTPOST

Dublin's fortunes were intimately bound up with the fortunes of the Anglo-Irish colony. As the colony declined and the administration became ever more ineffective, towns like Dublin became colonial outposts attempting to maintain their former status, at great cost to their citizens. Dublin's decline had been proceeding since at least the beginning of the fourteenth century, but in 1348, before the outbreak of the plague, there were indications that the city might recover from the downturn it had been experiencing. The Irish in Leinster were quiet, officials were being appointed regularly, revenue was being collected. But the plague's effects on the colony were such as to undo all that might have been recovered, and to cement the advantage that had been gained by the Gaelic-Irish. Because the plague so severely affected the city and surrounding villages, the city's security was affected. Expansionist-minded Gaelic-Irish lords took advantage of the disruption in the colony to mount raids, particularly on exposed manors in the Leinster area. The MicMhurchadha had proved to be a continuing security risk throughout the earlier decades of the century, but the years following the plague saw them stepping up the pressure, and the plague itself would seem to have provided the occasion for this. Since the MicMhurchadha territory lay high in the Wicklow hills, it was probably protected from the inroads of the plague. Dr Robin Frame stresses this point:

> The 1350s saw, from the crown's viewpoint, a further deterioration of security in Leinster, which seems to have been produced by the disproportionate impact of the Black Death upon the towns and nucleated settlements of the seaboard and river valleys.[42]

In the years after the plague the MacMhurchadha gained even more power in Wicklow and particularly in the area controlling the route from Dublin to the South. They succeeded in making travel to Dublin so hazardous that in 1361 the decision was made to shift the seat of the exchequer to Carlow. Throughout the 1350s they made alliances in an opportunistic fashion with other Irish chieftains, Anglo-Irish lords and with the administration in Dublin. By the end of the century Art MacMurchadha Caomhánach was claiming to be King of Leinster while at the same time maintaining his links with the Dublin administration, alternately raiding and negotiating. In short, by severely affecting the towns and villages of Leinster, the plague helped to give the advantage to the MicMhurchadha. Again, the plague did not initiate this development, but it added to the momentum that it had been gathering in the course of the fourteenth century.

However, thanks to the general economic contraction of the colony and the effects of the Black Death, the central Dublin administration did not have adequate revenue to withstand these attacks and in the 1350s was increasingly forced to call on individual localities for subsidies to support the Justiciar's army. Dublin was asked for subsidies in 1353, 1355, 1358 and later. These requests were deeply resented by the citizens who saw them as yet further evidence of the greed of English-born officials. This is now added to plague and general warfare in the colonists' own list of the causes of the crisis that they faced in the later decades of the fourteenth century. In 1360, the Great Council, in an urgent plea to the King for help, complained that because of the plague's effects on the English in Ireland as well as the incompetence of government officials, the King's liege men could no longer defend themselves, and the city's finances were being drained by the continual wars that had to be waged. Five years later in 1365 Ireland is again described as being '...sunk in the greatest wretchedness through the poverty and feebleness of his (the King's) people there...' [43]

By the later fourteenth century the need for royal intervention was pressing and between 1361 and 1376, five military expeditions were sent to Ireland. But Richard II's expeditions were so circumscribed as to be an admission of defeat. He did not intend to conquer the land in Gaelic hands or to reconquer those parts of the colony that had been seized by the Irish; his sole aim was to make Leinster and Dublin safe and otherwise to maintain the status quo as it existed in 1390. The only effective answer now was withdrawal, abandoning the marcher areas altogether, and creating a heavily-fortified nucleus around Dublin – the Pale. Dublin's isolation and vulnerable situation is highlighted by a report of 1435 which stated that the King's writ ran only in an area thirty miles in length and twenty in breadth throughout the counties of Dublin, Meath, Louth and Kildare; the rest was overrun by the King's enemies and rebels. [44]

The plague's toll on the towns and manors of the colony, and especially in Dublin, meant that the colonists were even more a minority than they had ever been. Nor were their numbers replenished by new colonists as English people now, thanks to the Black Death, had more extensive opportunities for work and land in England itself. The easy availability of land in post-plague England, together with the straitened finances of the crown, meant that Ireland was no longer an attraction for those seeking land and opportunity. As a consequence, the cultural character of the colonists gradually changed. As contact with England slowed, interaction between the colonists and the

Gaelic-Irish quickened. Many Anglo-Irish colonists intermarried with the Gaelic-Irish and were drawn within the reach of the Irish language and culture. This interaction was evident even in the heart of the colony in Dublin. One instance was the parliamentary permission granted in 1474-1476 to the Abbots of St Mary's and St Thomas' Abbeys and to the Prior of All Hallows to 'hold intercourse' with the Irish, to enter into contracts with them and even to become godfathers to their children.[45] Such relations meant that the cultural and political divide between the two communities was becoming blurred. Interaction worked in reverse order as the Gaelic-Irish were also brought within the sphere of Anglo-Irish influence, particularly evident in their increasing participation in trade.

Yet, assimilation was never total, particularly in Dublin, which attempted to limit the influx of Gaelic-Irish into the city and stressed its character as a community of 'liege men'. Demographically and economically depressed, the city nevertheless retained its place as the centre of the colony. Contracted though it was, the colony never disappeared completely, though it wasn't until the later sixteenth century, when England was again overpopulated, that another attempt was made to colonise Ireland fully. By that time too the threat of plague had passed and with it the crisis mortality that had so undermined the medieval Anglo-Irish colony.

CHAPTER FIVE

After 1348

For those alive in 1348, the Black Death seemed to herald the end of the world. Just as its advent was signalled for contemporaries by cataclysmic events, so too its aftermath was seen in apocalyptic terms. Friar Clyn in his annals recounted a vision of what would follow the plague:

> The lofty cedar of Lebanon shall be set ablaze, and Tripoli destroyed and Acre taken and Saturn will ambush Jove and the bat will put the duke of the bees to flight. Within fifteen years there will be one faith and one God, and the others will vanish away, the sons of Jerusalem will be delivered from captivity, a race will arise without a head. ... There will be many battles and great slaughter, fierce hunger and mortality, and

political upheaval; ...the eastern beast and the western lion will subjugate the whole world by their power; and for fifteen years there will be peace throughout the whole earth and an abundance of crops. Then all the faithful will pass to the Holy Land over the parted waters and the city of Jerusalem will be glorified and the Holy Sepulchre honoured by all. In this tranquillity there will be heard news of the Antichrist. Be watchful.[1]

Contrary to expectations, the crises posed by the Black Death were overcome. However, for the next 300 years people had to contend with recurring outbreaks of the plague which were the single, most significant effect of the Black Death and were crucial in delaying recovery. Some of these later outbreaks were mild, but from an epidemiological point of view they cannot be dismissed since mild forms of plague often developed into severe epidemics. The mortality during these subsequent outbreaks was not as disastrous or widespread as that of 1348; however it was chronic. Though more localized, and often ignored in the official records, their effects were nonetheless severe in those areas they affected and helped prolong the crisis mortality of the plague years. Moreover, studies have shown that these recurring outbreaks had a profound effect on slowing population recovery in Europe generally, above all since these later outbreaks affected not only mortality levels but also, given their particular impact on young people, fertility and replacement rates. These later outbreaks had a cumulative impact in slowing down population growth in Ireland at least until the seventeenth century.[2]

Of course, many questions have been raised about the origin and nature of these later outbreaks. Some argue that the plague became enzootic in the larger cities of late medieval Europe. Others contend that since infected brown rats die off in six to ten years and black rats in an even shorter span, the plague could not become enzootic in Europe and had to be reintroduced each time from disease reservoirs in central Asia. A recent study, however, has shown that the plague bacillus can persist even in very low rat populations, so that new outbreaks are not necessarily caused by the introduction of fresh supplies of the bacterium from outside foci. This would help explain the persistent outbreaks of plague, often on a very local level, and in places far removed from ports, throughout the later fourteenth and fifteenth centuries. There are also those questions as to whether the outbreaks of pestilence in England and Ireland in the fifteenth and sixteenth centuries were always outbreaks of bubonic plague. Shrewsbury, for example, argued that none of the later outbreaks offers a clinical description of bubonic plague, with the possible exception of an outbreak in the north-west of Ireland in 1478. He and others contend these later outbreaks in the British Isles were mixed and included smallpox, typhus fever, dysentery, anthrax, or some form of haemorrhagic viral disease. There is no doubt that a whole plethora of diseases were rife throughout the earlier part of the fifteenth century: typhus, diphtheria, measles, dysentery, tuberculosis, even cholera to name but a few. Tuberculosis, for example, is estimated to have been responsible for about 20% of all deaths in London in the non-plague years during the seventeenth century. The poet, William Langland, in *Piers the Ploughman* lists all the ills to which people were prey in the later Middle Ages:

... fevers and fluxes, coughs and seizures, cramps, toothaches, catarrhs and cataracts, scabby skin-diseases, boils, tumours, feverish agues, fits of madness, and countless other foul complaints... a host of cruel diseases... foul contagions... plagues and poxes.

Finally, there are those recent studies that cast doubt on whether any of the medieval oubreaks was caused by *Y. pestis* at all, and argue that some other, far more virulent pathogen was responsible.[3]

Whatever scientific explanation may yet emerge for the medieval epidemic, contemporaries had little doubt: all epidemics were regarded as 'pestilence' or 'plague' and were thought of together with famine. The fact that the Reformation litany of the Church of England included a prayer for deliverance from 'plague, pestilence and famine' highlights how these three continued to be linked in the public mind for centuries. This is also reflected in the popular French saying, '*après la famine, la peste domine*'. Since a final laboratory pronouncement on the precise nature of these past epidemics is not possible, or at least not as yet, perhaps Dr George Pye's pronouncement of 1721 is the best approach one could adopt to this question:

Plague differs from an epidemic disease, but in degree of violence only; and consequently any epidemic sickness, that rages with more than ordinary violence, and which occasions an extraordinary mortality amongst mankind, may be and is properly termed a pestilence, or the Plague.[4]

It should be noted however, that the Irish annals in record-ing outbreaks of pestilence in the fifteenth and sixteenth centuries maintain a distinction between deaths by 'plague' and deaths from other diseases such as smallpox or the sweating disease. In referring to the former, they use either the Latin *'pestilentia magna'*, or the Irish *'pláigh'* or even more often *'pláigh mór'* (great plague).

Unfortunately, the accounts of later fourteenth-century outbreaks in Ireland tend to be as skimpy as those for the Black Death of 1348. And as we move into the fifteenth century, it is clear that chroniclers and annalists report outbreaks very selectively, as plague lost its virulence and its novelty and became yet one more disaster among many. By the sixteenth and seventeenth centuries, record-keeping had advanced enough to offer us more details of how Dublin's authorities responded to outbreaks of epidemics. The accumulation of all the descriptions of these later outbreaks and the details they offer can, by analogy, offer another perspective on what may have happened in those hidden years of 1348-1350.

Cities in particular suffered from these later outbreaks, as in the later Middle Ages the plague became increasingly a regional and especially an urban phenomenon. Florence, for example, was hit by plague at least eight times between 1348 and 1427 and lost about two-thirds of its population of 100,000.[5] Dublin too suffered from repeated outbreaks throughout the rest of the fourteenth century and beyond. A further aggravation here was the continuing warfare in the Leinster area that affected so many aspects of life in the city. The combined effects of war and plague ensured a contin-uing decline in population that is borne out by the ongoing requests from the citizens for tax relief and murage grants.

The first major post-Black Death outbreak came in 1361, when the annalist of St Mary's Abbey, Dublin recorded a second major pestilence, 'consuming many men, but few women'. He then notes the death of Maurice Doncref, citizen of Dublin, who was buried in the Dominican cemetery, clearly a popular resting-place for Dublin's citizens. This is the plague that in the *Annals of Loch Cé* is referred to as '*Cluiche anrígh*' or 'The King's Game' and that is also recorded in the *Annals of Clonmacnoise* and the *Annals of the Four Masters*. In parts of England it was referred to as 'The King's Evil', and in *The Greatest Benefit to Mankind*, Roy Porter speculates that it was possibly an outbreak of scrofula or a scrofulous disease, which could reputedly be cured by royal touch. Whatever its precise nature, this outbreak severely affected parts of Co. Dublin. Mortality was high in the royal manors in the county, leaving vacant holdings in Crumlin, Saggard and Newcastle Lyons for which tenants could not be found. A number of chroniclers elsewhere made particular mention of the large numbers of children and young people who died during this outbreak. Henry Knighton, as well as the chronicler of Louth Park Abbey and numerous others all note that the plague killed young people and children especially, but also men and especially the wealthy.[6] The fact that particular mention is made of children and the wealthy is significant as studies elsewhere have shown that those sections of the population escaping the initial wave of plague were often affected in subsequent outbreaks.

This pattern also characterizes the description of the next outbreak of plague by the annalist at St Mary's Abbey. In 1370 he recorded a third plague which he described as '*maxima*', an epithet which he had also used to describe the outbreak

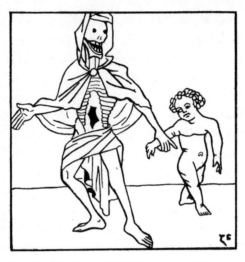

Death and the Young Child (German *c.*1465).

of 1348. During this outbreak, he wrote, 'many nobles, citizens and innumerable youths and children died'.[7] This tallies with reports from England that also noted the unusually high mortality among children. Why children were particularly affected is not known, but it casts doubt on the argument that immunity to plague could be inherited. Or conversely, those who had survived earlier plagues may have acquired immunity, in which case the death rate among those who had not been exposed – primarily children and young people - would be higher. Surviving evidence also indicates that later outbreaks of plague continued to affect the young primarily. A study done on parish registers in England in 1591-1592, for example, showed that up to 60% of plague deaths were of minors or children. The long-term demographic consequences were significant. High mortality among the young meant that a lower birth rate would continue for a long time. This, together with the recurrence of plague, meant that generations of children would never reach childbearing age, ensuring that a population's chances of recovering from plague mortality were further damaged. Figures from England indicate that life expectancy continued to decline: where the average life expectancy for those born in 1301-1325 was 29.8 years, this had dropped to 17.3 for those born in 1351-1375, and rose only slowly thereafter: 20.5 for 1376-1400, 23.8 for 1401-1425. There is no reason to suppose that conditions in Dublin were any different, particularly considering that the city was not being re-peopled from any other quarter.[8]

Between 1374 and 1379 a fourth pestilence is recorded in England, moving from south to north. Thomas Walsingham, in his *Historia Anglicana,* writes:

> The hand of God was so heavy on us that villages and towns, which had once been packed with warlike, provident and wealthy men, and with settlers, were emptied of their inhabitants and left desolate and abandoned.

There isn't any record of this plague in Ireland, though Thady Dowling's continuation of Clyn's *Annals of Ireland* records an outbreak in 1373. The next major outbreak of plague that is recorded was in 1383, when the *Annals of the Four Masters* and the *Annals of Clonmacnoise* note that a 'great and virulent plague raged universally throughout Ireland'. Harris, in his *History and Antiquities of the City of Dublin,* records a fourth pestilence also in this year, which destroyed an 'abundance of people' in the city. The outbreak also claimed victims in Trim, Laois, Wexford and Tipperary. Sometimes these plagues were so localized and so frequent as to be given only passing mention by the chroniclers.[9]

A fifth wave of plague is recorded in England between 1390 and 1393 and, according to Walsingham, it killed many but especially adolescents and children, 'who died in incredible numbers in towns and villages everywhere'. Plagues are also recorded in the Dublin area in the last decade of the century. Clyn's *Annals* record an outbreak in the Dublin area in 1391. One year later, the plague is reported to have had severe effects on the tenants of Colemanstown in the manor of Newcastle Lyons in Co. Dublin. Sixteen tenants died, leaving only three survivors, though the record is not altogether clear as to whether this is the mortality from just this one outbreak, or a cumulative mortality in the wake of a wave of plagues. Plagues are recorded in the English Pale when O'Brien Maol died of it in 1398 and two other notables a year later.[10]

Throughout the fifteenth century, plague broke out in different parts of Ireland at frequent intervals – approximately every decade. Plagues or plague deaths are recorded so frequently throughout the first half of the century – in 1401, 1406, 1408-1410, 1417-1419, 1422-1426, 1431, 1438-1439, 1446-1448 – that they must have become almost commonplace.[11] An outbreak in Dublin in 1424 killed Edmund Mortimer, Earl of March who had come to Ireland to lead a campaign against the Mic Murchadha in Wicklow whose raids on Dublin and surroundings had become a continual threat to the city's security. No other deaths are recorded, but given the nature of plague, even in its mildest bubonic form, others too must have died. Fifteen years later, in 1439, we are told thousands died when the plague broke out in Dublin: between the beginning of spring and the end of May over 3,000 people, male and female, young and old, died. Another outbreak in 1447 raged in Leinster, as well as in Munster and in Meath and killed a reported 700 priests. According to the annals of Dudley MacFirbis, 'it is difficult to get an accompt of the innumerable multitudes that died in Dublin of that plague'.[12] The *Annals of Connacht* record a 'great plague' in Dublin in 1466, as well as in nearby Meath and Leinster, and the *Annals of the Four Masters* record a great plague throughout the country in 1478, which according to Harris wasted Dublin in 1477. Further outbreaks or individual plague deaths are recorded in Dublin or throughout the country in the latter half of the century: in 1464, 1467, 1468, 1477-1478, 1484-1485, 1488 and 1498.[13]

An outbreak in 1489 had particularly severe effects on Dublin. The annalists record a general plague that was so great huge numbers died and people did not even bury the dead. Many citizens of Dublin died and parliament was postponed because people were afraid to enter the city, again another indication of the extent to which plague was perceived as an urban phenomenon. Measures then enacted indicate that, as in the rest of Europe, Dublin's authorities were now attempting to exercise control over the spread of plague by introducing public health regulations:

> The king has been informed that dungheaps, swine, pigsties and other nuisances in the streets, lanes and suburbs of Dublin infect the air and produce mortality, fevers and pestilence throughout the city. Many citizens and sojourners have thus

died in Dublin. The fear of pestilence prevents the coming thither of lords, ecclesiastics and lawyers. Great detriments thence arise to his majesty, as well as dangers to his subjects and impediments to his business. The king commands the mayor and bailiffs to cause forthwith the removal of all swine, and to have the streets and lanes free from ordure, so as to prevent loss of life from pestilential inhalations. The mayor is to expel all vagrants and mendicants from the city.[14]

These regulations do not indicate any change in people's understanding of the disease: smells, dirt and refuse were still seen as the originating causes of disease, beggars and vagrants as the most obvious agents of its dissemination. Ordinances were passed in 1366 forbidding the slaughter of animals within the city because of 'noxious and excessive stenches'. Enforcement cannot have been very effective as in the 1450s ordinances were still being passed governing the slaughter of animals and the disposal of waste.

Elsewhere, the care of the sick became increasingly a matter of public concern, and efforts were made to control the spread of disease by isolating plague victims. Hospitals became more common: in Venice and other Italian cities, for example, from the end of the fourteenth century pesthouses or *lazarettos* were built outside the walls of the city to isolate suspected plague victims. Health boards were established to implement public health measures, such as burying the plague dead in special pits, burning the possessions of plague victims and providing medical services to those afflicted with plague. These measures were first introduced in Italy and France but were not widely adopted in Germany until the early decades of the fifteenth century. They would not be introduced in Dublin until the later sixteenth century, though as in many parts of Europe, the systematic implementation of plague regulations did not become general until the beginning of the eighteenth century.[15]

To what extent were such measures successful, and did people's living conditions change in the fifteenth century? Evidence from mainland Europe indicates that the level of general nutrition improved, with coarse grains disappearing from the diet and more protein being consumed. This has been cited as a factor in the population increase in mainland Europe in the later part of the century, though demographers such as Livi-Bacci contend that improved diet does not appreciably effect a fall in mortality and that the great epidemic cycles operate independently of the state of nutrition. Moreover, it is not at all clear that diet improved considerably for urban populations in general. In the wake of the Black Death, the cost of food fell. However, in the longer term the income of urban workers did not rise, nor therefore their ability to buy more nutritious food. Moreover, Dublin experienced severe problems with the food supply that continued into the fifteenth century and the continuing migration of its citizens clearly indicates that standards of living did not appreciably improve.[16]

THE SIXTEENTH CENTURY

Whereas signs of recovery and of population growth became unmistakable in England by the second quarter of the sixteenth century, this was not to happen in Ireland for another century. The continuing outbreaks of plague, and the persistence of warfare and emigration prevented the city's population from making any sort of sustained recovery and in the sixteenth century Dublin continued to experience neglect and contraction. Because these later plagues are better documented, they afford another way of surmising what responses to earlier plagues could have been.

In an echo of the effects of the plague of 1348, a report on the outbreak of 1515 emphasizes the fact that the plague had destroyed the English, but not the Irish:

> the pestylens hathe devowred the Englysche folke, bycause they flee not therfro; and bycause the Irysche folke abyde not ther wyth, hyt do them noo hurt.

Studies have shown that in fact in the sixteenth and seventeenth centuries English forces in Ireland were often defeated by outbreaks of plague as well as of typhus. Not that the Irish were spared the plague completely. *The Annals of the Four Masters*, for example, record a great plague in east Fermanagh in 1520, 'of which many good men died'. This outbreak began in 1519 and lasted until 1525, but it was particularly devastating in the area around Dublin. *The Annals of Loch Cé* report that it killed 'a great number of the Foreigners' of Dublin. The Earl of Surrey had just arrived to take up the office of Lord Lieutenant when the plague erupted, but unlike many of his fellow administrators who fled, he decided to remain in the city with his family. The plague continued in the area of the Pale throughout the summer and autumn of 1520. Writing from Dublin on 3 August 1520, the Earl described it thus:

> There is a marvellous death in all this country, which is so sore that all the people be fled out of their houses into the fields and woods, where they likewise die wonderfully, so that their bodies be dead like swine unburied.

The outbreak continued at sporadic intervals into 1523 and 1524.[17]

A decade later, in 1535, towns throughout the Pale and especially Dublin and its surroundings were again devastated. The rebellion of Silken Thomas or Thomas Fitzgerald, son of the ninth earl of Kildare, in June 1534 took place against the background of plague in the city. According to Harris' *History and Antiquities of the City of Dublin* the city was 'much dispeopled' during this outbreak. Not only had the citizens themselves fled, many had sent their children to school in the country 'to avoid the inconveniences of the plague'. Fitzgerald took advantage of the plague to kidnap some of these children and hold them to ransom. However, his ruse did not succeed, the citizens rallied their strength and forces and Silken Thomas was forced to retreat. The dissolved monastery of All Hallows was subsequently awarded to the citizens by a grateful King. For the next two years epidemics raged in Ireland, though again their precise cause is not clear. Continuing outbreaks such as these throughout his kingdom led Henry VIII to issue a general order on the subject of plague in 1543, endorsing measures that were already in force in Continental Europe. Those afflicted with plague or any who had come into contact with them were to isolate themselves for forty days, the usual period of quarantine; the bedding and clothing of infected people was to be burned; all dogs 'other than hounds, spaniels or mastiffs, necessary for the custody or safe keeping of their houses' were to be killed; all common beggars were to be kept out of churches; all streets and lanes had to be cleaned. To ensure that this order would reach the widest audience, the King ordered it to be read in churches throughout his kingdom.[18] As the century progressed, measures such as these would be made even more stringent and enforced more rigorously.

By the time of the next major outbreak of plague in 1574, Dublin had expanded and clearly improvements had been made. A contemporary account describes it as:

> the royal city of Ireland, its most notable mart and chief seat of justice, defended with strong walls, adorned with beautiful buildings and well-peopled with inhabitants.[19]

But change was perhaps restricted. Richard Stanihurst in 1577 in a eulogy to his native city echoes this praise, noting its superior manners and civility, its fresh water, its proximity to the countryside, and its people's hospitality; but he also notes that beggars swarmed there daily and made 'the whole city in effect their hospital'. The leper and other hospitals that in the previous century had been operated by the religious orders had been closed during the dissolution of the monasteries. No other network of hospitals had been established in their place, so that the sick poor had few facilities. The city's poorer quarters still offered the cramped and unhygienic conditions suitable for the transmission of plague and disease.

A severe outbreak of plague in summer 1574 had severe consequences for Dublin. It subsided with the onset of the winter, but reappeared in the spring of 1575. An entry in the *Annals of the Four Masters* describes its appearance:

> Intense heat and extreme drought in the summer of this year; there was no rain for one hour, by night or day, from Bealtaine to Lammas. A loathsome disease and a dreadful malady arose from this heat, namely the plague. This malady raged violently among the Irish and English in Dublin, in Naas of Leinster, Ardee, Mullingar and Athboy. Between those

places, many a castle was left without a guard, many a flock without a shepherd, and many a noble corpse without a burial, in consequence of this distemper.

Another annalist, Thady Dowling, describes the devastation:

The City of Dublin was as if deserted of people, so that grass grew in the streets and at the doors of churches; no term was held after Trinity, and prayers were appointed by the Archbishop throughout the whole province.[20]

Between June and October 1575, a contemporary estimate of some 'three thousand men at least' died in the city, or about one-third of the city's estimated population. This time business as usual was not possible and parliament was moved to Drogheda. The wealthy and powerful fled at the first sign of plague. Clontarf and especially Dalkey were among the retreats most favoured by Dubliners, and one report has it that Dalkey Island 'was covered with the tents of the refugees while the sickness continued'. By June of that year, so many aldermen, officials and wealthy residents had fled that the city's authorities were forced to take action. The mayor ordered those who had fled either to return or send a deputy to carry out their responsibilities: the penalty for non-compliance was to be permanent deprivation of their citizenship. The city authorities provided temporary pesthouses on the outskirts of the city 'for the reliefe of the infected', though these were also intended to isolate the victims from the rest of the population. One such pesthouse was to be built in the 'great gardinge in Allhallowes nowe in the occupacion of William Stuoks shoemaker', formerly the monastery of All Hallows. Provisions were also made for the appointment of guardians of the pesthouses, who were to be 'honnest house hold-ers' whose job was 'to keape the seyke foulkes'. Clearly, people attempted to hide infected family members from the notice of the authorities as another regulation required citizens to notify the authorities of any outbreak within twenty-four hours, or else risk imprisonment for eighty days and banishment from the city. And a city physician was appointed with specific responsibility for victims of the plague. The Council ruled that:

> Denis Collier, phisician and surgien shalbe and is admitted to the fraunches, fryudomes and libertyes of the cittie of Dublin in consideration that he nowe adventured his life in this con-tagious tyme of plague into the cittye, attendyng upon the Maire and every other that shalbe in danger or neede of phisicke or surgrye; that he shall continue during his life in service of the cittie, as well in the tyme of plague as in all other tymes, doyng his duety, taking for his [fee] as the patient and he shall agree, or as the Maire for the tyme being shall ressonablye order or adward.

Further, the city authorities in 1578 appointed an official, one Barnaby Rathe, as Master of the Beggars with special respon-sibility for 'kyllinge such swine as he shall fynde in the streets, and rydinge the cittie of vacabonds and beggars'. The prob-lem of vagabonds and beggars is systematically addressed throughout England and Ireland from the first half of the six-teenth century. Increasingly distinctions were made between 'sturdy' or 'valiant' beggars, that is beggars who were able-bodied and capable of working, who were banished and the sick poor, for whom provisions were willingly made[21].

THE SEVENTEENTH CENTURY AND
THE END OF THE PLAGUE

Dublin was again visited by plague in 1604-1605 and the responses of its citizens follow the patterns that had been established in the previous century. The wealthy again fled to safe areas, leaving the remaining citizens complaining and threatening to strip them of their citizenship unless they, or their deputies, returned to discharge their duties. This anger with 'runaways' was common in other cities at this time; in contemporary London during the great Plague of 1625, for example, the writer Thomas Dekker castigated the wealthy who fled the city leaving the poor 'in sorrow, in sickness, in penury, in unpitied disconsolations'. In Dublin, ordinances were passed requiring that henceforth any householder wishing to leave the city had to have a license from the mayor. Plague victims were to be segregated in a pesthouse outside the city in George's Lane and four men were hired to manage the house and bury the dead. They were also enjoined to '...stop the infected from running abrode', a reference to the delirium experienced by patients in the advanced stages of plague which caused them to run into the streets and no doubt contributed in no small measure to the panic and unease of the citizens. In the first mention of a *cordon sanitaire*, only those coming from a plague-free area were to be allowed into the city. Preventative measures were also required. Citizens were ordered to light fires before their doors three nights a week in order to purge the air and thereby prevent the transmission of disease:

It is agreed that, for better purgeing of the aire, Mr Maior do command that every inhabitant shall burn a fagot at his dore every Wednesday at night, Satterday at night, and Monday at night, and other such nights as Mr Maior shall thinke fit, and occasion shall happen.

Frontispiece from Thomas Dekker, *A Rod for Run-awayes* (1625), warning that nobody can escape the plague, not even those who flee the city.

Whether this practice had been widely adopted during earlier outbreaks is a question. There are contemporary images from 1348 of the Avignon Pope, Clement VI, locking himself indoors and positioning himself for the duration of the plague between two fires. Finally, in an effort to control the ongoing problems posed by the large numbers of beggars and vagrants who thronged into the city from the country and were seen as responsible for spreading contagion among the citizens, the Corporation was petitioned to erect a 'Bridewell or house of correction and labour'. These measures were in line with measures already introduced in England and Scotland; in Edinburgh, for example, infected families were removed to moors outside the towns, their houses disinfected and two men were charged with enforcing pest regulations.[22]

By the time of the last major outbreak of plague in Ireland in 1650, much had changed. The years after 1641 had brought famine, plague, war and depopulation. Trade slumped, food had to be imported and the limited recovery of the early decades of the seventeenth century had disappeared. The religious houses, which formerly had cared for the poor and sick had been suppressed, and the responsibility of caring for victims of the plague now rested with the civic authorities. This last outbreak coincided with Cromwell's campaign in Ireland and contributed in no small measure to his success by helping to weaken the defences of those towns which resisted his advances. The fact that the winter was a mild one facilitated the spread of the plague, as has also been surmised for the outbreak of 1348, though one should note Shrewsbury's contention that this 'plague' could well have been an outbreak of malignant dysentery, typhus fever or haemorrhagic smallpox.

This time the epidemic probably started on the west coast in Galway, brought there probably by ship from Spain. Within nine months '...many thousand soules died of the said sickness'. It had broken out in Kilkenny by March 1650, and had caused 'immense mortality' by the time Cromwell had reached the city. Waterford was stricken by late April and by spring 1651, the plague had reached Limerick. Overall, probably about one third of the population of Ireland died in the plague of the 1650s and a contemporary account forecast that 'the plague will devour what the sword has not in Ireland'.[23]

In terms that echo what we know of the effects of the plague of 1348, the plague of 1650 was reported to have 'exceedingly depopulated' the city of Dublin. Half of its houses were destroyed, and the rest fell into ruin. Nor could they be repaired because of the severe mortality among craftsmen and workmen. Aldermen who had fled the city were dismissed. Petitions from the Commons of Dublin to the General Assembly stressed the need for poor relief, subsidies to the pesthouse and aid in burying the dead. However, in a by now familiar cry, they stressed that raising taxes was not the answer:

> it is not convenient to lay a cesse on the cittie at present, by reason of the absence of the able inhabitants of this cittie and the greate mortalitie.

On 7 June 1653 a committee was appointed which would meet weekly. Its duties included providing for the poor and for plague victims, erecting a pesthouse where necessary and doing everything possible 'in order to aid in the prevention of the increase of the contagion'.[24]

Doctor with mask. In the early 1600s doctors began to wear a robe coated with wax to prevent the 'seeds' of disease from adhering to it. The beak was a kind of breathing tube filled with perfumed material to keep 'pestilent air' at bay. In fact the wearing of a mask helps to prevent the transmission of pneumonic plague and is still recommended for use by those who come in contact with plague victims.

However, the understanding of disease had still not changed significantly from what had been known a century before. Medical men had admittedly become more prominent and more confident in their ability to deal with plague. John Sterne, a Meath doctor who had trained at Oxford and Cambridge, gained kudos for his work during the plague of 1651 in Dublin and in 1662 was made a professor of physic at Trinity College. One might here note also Niall O'Glacan of Donegal, who trained in Ireland and abroad, and who was a professor in the Universities of Toulouse and Bologna, physician to the King of France and who in 1629 published a treatise on pestilence, *Tractatus de Peste*. Nevertheless, despite the expertise, the belief in the miasmatic origin of epidemics continued into the nineteenth century. In 1721, a Dublin doctor, Richard Boulton, wrote that epidemic disease was caused by an 'External Disposition of the Air' and 'an Internal Disposition of the Humours'. Even the spread of typhus, which in the nineteenth century overtook plague as the dominant killer, was attributed to tainted air polluting the houses of rich and poor alike.[25]

Many others still understood the prime causes of the plague in terms that did not differ significantly from those cited in 1348. A conference of Catholic bishops in 1649 saw the outbreak of plague as an expression of God's anger with the Irish nation. In one of his plague pamphlets about the plague in London, *A Rod for Runawayes*, Thomas Dekker in around 1625 also blamed it on God's anger:

> For, Iehouah, when he is angry, holds three Whips in his hand, and neuer drawes bloud with them, but when our Faults are heauy, our Crimes hainous: and those three Whips are, the sword, pestilence and famine.

THE

Seuen Deadly Sinnes

of London :

Drawn in seuen seuerall Coaches,
Through the seuen seuerall Gates of the
Citie

Bringing the Plague with them.

Opus septem Dierum.

Tho : Dekker.

At London
Printed by *E.A.* for *Nathaniel Butter,* and are to bee sold
at his shop neere Saint Austens gate.
1606.

Frontispiece from Thomas Dekker, *Seven Deadly Sins:*
The connection between sin and plague is still stressed
in the seventeenth century.

Oliver Cromwell saw the outbreak of plague in Kilkenny in 1650
as God's judgement on a sinful city and a sign of his own elec-
tion by God. However, this did not save General Ireton, chief
commander of his army in Ireland, nor a large part of his army,
from dying of plague. A petition from the citizens of Dublin in
1657 blamed the plague on public immorality, specifically on
cursing:

there is very much of sweareinge, curseinge and blasphemie used and practised (as in the English tongue too much soe also in the Irish tongue), which as it is a breach of the good lawes of the land, soe it is a high provokeinge of God which may justly cause the plague and other judgements to sease uppon this cittie.[26]

Nor had public health conditions changed radically. Throughout the seventeenth century, complaints were still being made about the dirty streets, the roaming pigs and the numerous beggars with infectious diseases, all of which were seen to corrupt the air and endanger the health of the citizens of Dublin.[27] A report published in 1653, *A Declaration touching the Poor*, highlights the poverty of the city:

Some feed on carrion and weeds, some starve on the highways, poor children deserted or exposed by their parents are fed on by ravenous wolves and beasts and birds of prey. All means of stopping this must be tried. Impotent people are to be assisted and able-bodied vagrants sent to houses of correction till they are broken from their idle course of life, and willing to betake themselves to some honest calling. At present the number is too large, and the poverty of the country too great to effectually put the law in force.[28]

This was the last major outbreak of the plague in Dublin, and despite its devastation, the city recovered quickly this time. Ireland's economy picked up gradually, and in the second half of the century Dublin particularly profited from the country's economic expansion, becoming the largest city in Ireland and the second largest in the British Isles. The city's population increased significantly, thanks largely to the cessation of major epidemics and to immigration. Its population in 1600 has been estimated as having been somewhere between 5,000 and about 10,000; by 1660 this had increased to between 25,000 and 30,000, doubled again in the next twenty years and increased more slowly thereafter. Its old medieval walls were knocked down, indicating that the city had expanded and developed in a way not seen since the thirteenth century. In the succeeding decades, Dutch refugees in Dublin helped to repair the city's dwellings and the timber-framed houses of medieval times were gradually replaced by tall, narrow houses of brick and stone, known as 'Dutch Billyies', in honour of their builders. By this time too Dublin had become definitively an outpost of English culture and a colonial capital.[29]

The effect of the plague experience on the government of cities and on public health policies was profound. Though the causes and transmission of plague were – and still are – imperfectly understood, the human response to plague helped bring about improved public health and sanitation, better nutrition and housing, and advances in medical knowledge, all of which helped to contain the worst ravages of other epidemics in Europe's cities in later centuries. Public health officials embarked on the measures that would be continued for the next five centuries until bubonic plague had become a very localized threat: replacing wooden houses with stone, providing more adequate, covered sewage, ensuring a clean water supply, erecting pesthouses, controlling the rat population and rubbish disposal. Many decades more were to elapse before the epidemiology of bubonic plague was fully understood. In San Francisco, for example, during the 1900 outbreak authorities designated plague as a 'rice-eaters' disease' that was peculiar to Asians and to those with whom they had contact. Only with the 1907 outbreak and the understanding of the role of the rat in the transmission of *Y. pestis* were cities like San Francisco finally able to take the appropriate measures to contain the epidemic. However, Dublin remained backward in the area of public health. The River Liffey remained the city's main sewer and proposals for sewage treatment plants were met with resistance from ratepayers who saw them as 'fads'. With continuing complaints about pigs foraging in lanes and occasionally attacking people, slaughter houses and pig sties within the city, inadequate sanitation and contaminated water supplies, Dublin was widely regarded as one of the unhealthiest major cities in Ireland and Britain until the early twentieth century. Not until the Public Health Act of 1848 did Dublin Corporation achieve any authority in regard to public health.[30]

From the mid-seventeenth century, outbreaks of the plague in Ireland, as well as in Europe generally, became increasingly rare, though they recurred periodically in Europe until 1894 and a case of plague was officially reported in Ireland as late as 1920.[31] However, the days of the widespread epidemics of the medieval plague were over, to be replaced by epidemics of other diseases, especially typhus. Whether or not public health measures were responsible for the eradication of plague is of course, as already noted, now a matter of renewed and continuing debate. Some have suggested that the reason for the plague's diminution may be that rats acquired immunity and therefore the disease-ridden flea no longer had to abandon its host. Another cause cited is the replacement of the black rat by the less human-friendly brown rat. Others point to the increasing domestication of rats, as with improved housing and food storage in western countries rats did not migrate as they used, and so the plague remained restricted. The increasing use of stone in building materials was a factor. So was the growing acceptance and understanding of the notion of contagion which led public authorities to set up pesthouses, impose quarantine procedures on ships, merchants and even entire towns, burn the belongings and even houses of plague victims, and clean up urban environments. Changing trade routes meant the eclipse of ports such as Venice and Marseilles through which the plague had entered Europe in the medieval period, and with the increasing importance of the North Sea ports the link with endemic foci of the plague in the East was broken. And at the Venice Convention of 1897 the European Powers agreed to pool their information on outbreaks of plague in their territories and to notify one another as soon as plague broke out, a move that did much to contain the spread of plague. Later again the use of antibiotics helped to reduce plague, at least of the bubonic variety, to a minor, treatable illness.[32]

However, none of these explanations has proved entirely satisfactory, as is evidenced in the ongoing debates about the plague and its causes. Many scientists now argue for biological changes in the balance of pathogen-rat-flea, speculating that there is a tide in the affairs of disease over which human beings have no control. In this story the human is but an accidental victim. McNeill in his history of epidemics argued that '...there are natural rhythms at work that limit and define the demographic consequences of sudden exposure to initially very lethal infections' and that after five or six human generations, the disease had played itself out. It is a view echoed by Hans Zinsser in his work on the subject, *Rats, Lice and History*:

> Nothing in the world of living things is permanently fixed...
> On purely biological grounds, therefore, it is entirely logical to
> suppose that infectious diseases are constantly changing; new
> ones are in the process of developing, and old ones being mod-
> ified or disappearing.

Livi-Bacci also concurs: 'For reasons not entirely clear the plague underwent a process of mutual adaptation between pathogen (*Yersinia*), carrier (flea) and host–victim (human)'. Perhaps rats and humans developed a resistance, or perhaps the microbe itself changed. Other theories abound. Recent research has focused on the hypothesis that populations exposed to plague acquired immunity to it and genetic researchers speculate about a link between the gene, known as CCR5, which confers protection against HIV, and the possibility that that same gene variant may have arisen in Europe as a direct response to the Black Death. The possible reasons for the eclipse of the plague in early modern Europe then are many, and most likely lie beyond the doings of human beings. Whatever the cause, plague had all but disappeared from European towns by the early eighteenth century and with it the crisis mortality that had kept population levels so low throughout the medieval period.[33]

Yet plague has not disappeared from the human landscape. Today it is endemic in various places: Madagascar, East Africa, Brazil, Peru, Myanmar, Vietnam, India, the south–western United States, on the edges of the Caspian Sea and the eastern slopes of the Caucasus. According to the World Health Organisation, between 1954 and 1997 plague affected thirty-eight countries worldwide, and led to 80,613 cases and 6,587 fatalities. These latter-day outbreaks are different to the medieval plague in that they occur mostly in rural areas and small rural villages and case fatality is generally about 14%. Fatality, however, was much higher when it was used as a weapon of biological warfare, as for example by Japan in China during the Second World War. Both the bubonic and pneumonic strains of plague remain in the arsenal of biological weaponry. In 1970, the World Health Organisation estimated that fifty kilos of *Y. pestis* disseminated in an aerosol cloud over a city of five million people could result in 150,000 cases of pneumonic plague, 36,000 of whom would be expected to die despite medical attention.[34]

Exceptional circumstances aside, bubonic plague has become a largely rural, extremely localized phenomenon. Or so we hope. For, as Zinsser and MacNeill warned, nothing remains static in the story of the microbe and, in 1997, the *New England Journal of Medicine* reported a case of multiple antibiotic-resistant plague. As one medical authority notes:

Plague is an ancient disease that is not likely to disappear; its continued outbreaks throughout the world attest to its tenacious presence... The quiescent periods, during which few or no human cases are detected, may last for years, leading to mistaken declarations of plague eradication. However long the silent periods last, plague may suddenly reappear. The combination of false assurance of its eradication, and the failure of public health vigilance, sets the stage for the panic that may ensue when enzootic plague spills over from its natural cycle into the peridomestic and commensal rodent populations (and their fleas), bringing plague into closer human contact. Poor sanitation, overcrowding and high numbers of rodents are conditions that enhance urban plague transmission.[35]

Scientists continue to speculate on the nature and origin of the pathogen that ravaged Europe in the Middle Ages. In 2001, the bacterium *Y. pestis* was sequenced, based on a sample taken from a veterinarian who died of the plague in Colorado in 1992, and its development mapped.[36] Researchers found 149 genes that once enabled the bacterium to survive in the human gut, but which are now deactivated. They also discovered that it had changed rapidly in a relatively short span – in biological terms – from a harmless bacterium that used to cause gastroenteritis into the deadly bacterium it became in the Middle Ages, and then again to the relatively harmless disease it is today.

Much remains to be known about the plague and its effects on fourteenth-century Dubliners, on late medieval Europeans and on human society in general. However, one fact remains clear: in the long, slow march of bacterial life, humans play but a minor role.

Abbreviations

Notes

Bibliography

List of Illustrations

Index

Abbreviations

AC	*Annals of Connacht 1224-1544*
AFM	*Annals of the Kingdom of Ireland by the Four Masters*
AI	*Annals of Innisfallen*
ALC	*Annals of Loch Cé*
Anal. Hib.	Analecta Hibernica
Ann. Clon.	*Annals of Clonmacnoise*
AU	*Annals of Ulster*
Cal. Alen's Reg.	*Calendar of Archbishop Alen's Register*
Cal. Close Rolls	*Calendar of the Close Rolls*
Cal. Doc. Ire.	*Calendar of Documents Relating to Ireland, 1171-1307*
Cal. Justic. Rolls	*Calendar of the Justiciary Rolls of Ireland*
Cal. Pat. Rolls	*Calendar of Patent Rolls*
CARD	*Calendar of the Ancient Records of Dublin*
CELT	*Corpus of Electronic Texts Online,* University College Cork
Chart. St. Mary's	*Chartularies of St. Mary's Abbey, Dublin and Annals of Ireland 1162-1370*
Clyn, Annals	*Annals of Ireland by Friar John Clyn and Thady Dowling*
CPL	*Calendar of Entries in the Papal Registers relating to Great Britain and Ireland: Papal Letters*
CPP	*Calendar of Entries in the Papal Registers relating to Great Britain and Ireland: Papal Petitions*
Hist. & Mun. Docs. Ire.	*Historic and Municipal Documents of Ireland, 1172-1320*

Horrox	Horrox, R., (trans. and ed.), *The Black Death*
Ir. Geog.	*Irish Geography*
IHS	*Irish Historical Studies*
JRSAI	*Journal of the Royal Society of Antiquaries of Ireland*
NHI	*A New History of Ireland* ii.: *Medieval Ireland 1169-1534*, A. Cosgrove (ed.). iii. *Early Modern Ireland, 1534-169*, Moody et al. (eds.)
PRIA	*Proceedings of the Royal Irish Academy*
PRI Rep. D.K.	*Reports of the Deputy Keeper of the Public Records in Ireland*
PROI	*Public Record Office of Ireland*
Reg. Kilmainham	*Registrum de Kilmainham*
Reg. All Hallows	Registrum Prioratus Omnium Sanctorum juxta Dublin
SPD	*Calendar of State Papers and Letters, Domestic Series*

Notes

1: IN SEARCH OF THE BLACK DEATH

1 *Chart. St Mary's Abbey*, ii. cxviii; see also cxi-cxl; 'Chronicle of Pembridge', in *Black Book of Christ Church*; Mac Niocaill, 'The colonial town', 377.

2 Livi-Bacci, *The Population of Europe*, 70-75. In the following discussion, I have relied on: Biraben, *Les hommes et la peste en France et dans les pays européens et méditerranéens*, i. 7-21, 333-7; Dols, *The Black Death in the Middle East*, 68-83; Herlihy, *The Black Death*, 17-38; Hirst, *The Conquest of Plague*; Hollingsworth, *Historical Demography*, 355-75; Horrox, *The Black Death*, 3-13; Shrewsbury, *History of Bubonic Plague*, 1-6; Twigg, *The Black Death*; Watts, *Epidemics and History*, 1-6; WHO Plague Manual: *Epidemiology, Distribution, Surveillance, and Control*.

3 Parkhill, 'Genome sequence of *Yersinia pestis*, the causative agent of plague', 525.

4 Simpson, *A Treatise on Plague*, 97.

5 Raoult, et al., 'Suicide PCR/*Yersinia Pestis* as cause of the Black Death', 12800-12803.

6 Paterson, R., '*Yersinia* seeks pardon for the Black Death', 323; www.psu.edu/ur/2002/blackdeath

7 Livi-Bacci, *A Concise History*, 53. See Campbell, 'Population pressure', 127; Herlihy, *The Black Death*, 39; Gottfried, *The Black Death*, 4.

8 Schofield, et al. (ed.), *The Decline of Mortality*, 9, 14-17.

9 Gransden (ed.), *Historical Writing in English*, ii. 172-3; *Liber primus Kilk.*, 11-12; *Cal. Close Rolls*, 1343-6, p. 672.

10 *Hist. & Mun. Docs*, 62, 126; Warburton, *et al.*, *History of the City of Dublin*, i. 174-5; see Clarke, '*Urbs et suburbium*', 53ff.

11 Healy, 'The town walls of Dublin', 183; Simms, A., 'Origins and early growth', 42, 50-52 and Medieval Dublin: 'A topographical analysis', 38; Twigg, *The Black Death*, 100-101.

12 Clarke, '*Urbs et suburbium*', 45-58; Hennessy, 'The priory and hospital of New Gate', 42ff.; Otway-Ruthven, 'The medieval church lands of County Dublin', 54-72; Simms, A., 'Origins and early growth', 52-3.

13 Otway-Ruthven, 'The character of the Anglo-Norman settlement', 75-84; Russell, 'Late thirteenth-century Ireland', 500-512; Graham, 'The towns of medieval Ireland', 45; Hollingsworth, *Historical Demography*, 269-70, 364; Mac Niocaill, 'Socio-economic problems of the medieval town', 18-19.

14 Cited Meinsma, *De Zwarte Dood*, 303; Barry, *The Archaeology of Medieval Ireland*, 125, 138; see Pounds, *An Economic History of Medieval Europe*, 141-3.

15 Little, *Religious Poverty and the Profit Economy*, 22-3; van Werveke, 'The rise of the towns', 18-19; Russell, 'Late ancient and medieval population', 101-7, 110-112 and 'Population in Europe', 25-70; Pounds, *Historical Geography*, 329, 350-51; Gottfried, *The Black Death*, 42-76; Keen, *English Society*, 79; Smith, 'Demographic developments', 50, n.69; Jordan, *The Great Famine*, 128, n.14, 129ff.; Hollingsworth, *Historical Demography*, 364.

16 Twigg, *The Black Death*, 86-8; *Hist. & Mun. Docs.*, 256, 262-3.

17 *Hist. & Mun. Docs.*, 365; 282; *Liber Primus Kilk.*, 5, 6, 13.

18 Wallace, 'The archaeology of Anglo-Norman Dublin', 388ff.; Barry, *The Archaeology of Medieval Ireland*, 122.

19 Arrizabalaga, 'Facing the Black Death', 253-6, 275-7; Rawcliffe, *Medicine and Society*, 42-3.

20 CARD, i. 145, 298, 306, 327; ii. 92, 96, 101, 139, 370, 382.

21 Cited Ziegler, *The Black Death*, 159; *Hist. & Mun. Docs.* 253.

22 See Wallace, 'Recent discoveries at Wood Quay', 24 and 'The archaeology of Anglo-Norman Dublin', 390; Barry, *The Archaeology of Medieval Ireland*, 91, 121-2; Ó Ríordáin, 'Excavations at High St and Winetavern St, Dublin', 76 and 'The High Street excavations', 171ff.; Coughlan, 'The Anglo-Norman houses of Dublin', 232.

23 Gilbert, *History of the City of Dublin*, i. 298; *Cal. Alen's Reg*, 175.

24 Meyer, 'Pneumonic plague', 249-61; Dols, *The Black Death*, 74; Simpson, *A Treatise*, 182ff.

25 Coope, 'Report on the coleoptera from an eleventh-century house at Christ Church Place, Dublin', 56; *The Correspondence of Erasmus: Letters 1523-4*, p. 471; Gransden, *Historical Writing*, ii. 172.

26 Biraben, *La peste*, i. 12, 15, 130-1; Kelly, *A History of the Black Death*, 19.

27 Livi-Bacci, *The Population of Europe*, 41; Schofield, et al. (ed.), *Decline of Mortality*, 10-11; Perrenoud, 'The attenuation of mortality crises', 20; Rotberg & Rabb, *Hunger and History*, 308; Van Bath, *Agrarian History*, 84; cf. Duby, *Rural Economy*, 286.

28 Simpson, *A Treatise*, 184, Livi-Bacci, *Population and Nutrition*, 36, also 140ff;

Lunn, 'Nutrition', 137; Walter & Schofield, 'Famine', 18-21; Herlihy, *Black Death*, 4.

29 Jordan, *The Great Famine*, 186-7; Razi, *A Medieval Parish*, 107-9, 129-134.

30 AI, 371; AC, 157; Clyn, *Annals*, 9; *Chart. St Mary's Abbey*, ii. 290, 317; 'The Black Book of Christ Church' ed. Gwynn, 337.

31 Clyn, *Annals*, 10; *Chart. St Mary's Abbey*, ii. 323, 339, 295-6, 354, 358, 375; Joyce, *Ulysses*, 45.

32 *Hist. & Mun. Docs.*, 353-4, lxxii.

33 Barry, *The Archaeology of Medieval Ireland*, 124; Mitchell, *The Irish Landscape*, 191-2; see Ó Ríordáin, 'Excavations at High Street and Winetavern Street, Dublin', 77.

34 Mac Giolla Phádraig, 'Fourteenth-century life in a Dublin monastery', 116-7; Hoagland, *1000 Years of Irish Poetry*, 313; Heuser (ed.), *Die Kildare-Gedichte*, 146.

35 Hatcher, 'Mortality in the fifteenth century', 19-38; Livi-Bacci, *Population of Europe*, 57, 61 and Population and Nutrition, 64-5; Russell, 'Late ancient and medieval populations', 31; Power, 'A medieval demographic sample', 66-7.

36 Knighton, *Chronicle*, 97.

37 Lamb, *Climate, History and the Modern World*; Bailey, 'Per impetum maris', 186-206; Biraben, *La peste*, i. 134-9; Simpson, *A Treatise*, 140-2, 150; Twigg, *The Black Death*, 113, 114ff; Gottfried, *The Black Death*, 9.

38 Weikinn, *Quellenkunde zur Witterungsgeschichte Europas von der Zeitwende bis zum Jahre 1850*, Vol.1; E. Leroy Ladurie, *Times of Feast, Times of Famine*; Lyons, 'Weather, famine, pestilence and plague in Ireland, 900-1500', pp. 40-42, 63-6.

39 AC, 241, 253; *Chart. St Mary's Abbey*, ii. 362, 372-3, 381 (trans. cxxxv-cxxxvi); see also Dixon, 'Weather in old Dublin', part i. 94, part ii. 66ff.

40 Horrox, 54, 160-161; Meinsma, *De Zwarte Dood*, 303; Clyn, *Annals*, 38.

41 *Hist. & Mun. Docs.*, 74-5, 533, 521-3; *Chart. St Mary's Abbey*, ii. 290, 332.

42 *Cal. Archbishop's Alen Register*, 194.

43 *Hist. & Mun. Docs.*, 392-3, 405; Connolly, 'List of Irish Material', 52-3; *Cal. Pat. Rolls, 1330-1334*, p. 552-3; *Stat. Ire. John-Henry V*, 332-63; *Cal. Close Rolls, 1341-3*, pp.509-16.

44 *Hist. & Mun. Docs.*, 391-2, 456-62; *Cal. Archbishop Alen's Register*, 195; *Cal. Pat. Rolls*, 1330-34, p. 551.

45 *Chart. St Mary's Abbey*, ii. 361; *Cal. Close Rolls 1343-6*, p. 672; *Liber Primus Kilk*, 11; *Cal. Close Rolls 1339-41*, p. 244; *Cal. Close Rolls, 1346-9*, p. 77.

46 *Chart. St Mary's Abbey*, ii. 383-4, 388, cxxxvi-cxxxvii.

47 CPL, iii. 224, 227, 231, 253.

48 *History of Medieval Ireland*, 267; see also Frame, *The English Lordship in Ireland*, 132-9.

2: THE PLAGUE'S PROGRESS

1 AFM, i. 9; Dinneen (ed.), *Foclóir Gaedhilge agus Béarla: An Irish-English Dictionary, 1169-70*; Joyce, *The Origin and History of Irish Names of Places*, i. 162.

2 Shrewsbury, *History*, 20-21; MacArthur, 'Identification of some pestilences recorded in the Irish annals', 174-81; Biraben, *La peste*, i. 32; Simpson, *A Treatise*, 17ff.; Fleetwood, *History of Medicine in Ireland*, 16. On recent theories, see above, Chapter 1, pp.

3 AFM, i. 183, 275-6; Bede, *Ecclesiastical History*, 313.

4 ALC, i. 289; *A.I.*, 371; Clyn, *Annals*, 9, 10; *Chart. St Mary's Abbey*, ii. 290, 317, 323, 378; Flower, (ed.), 'The Kilkenny chronicle', 334.

5 On the plague's progress, see Dols, *The Black Death*, 35-55; Biraben, *La peste*, i. 48-55, 71-85.

6 Knighton, *Chronicle*, 98-9.

7 Clyn, *Annals*, 35ff; *Annals of Nenagh*, 160-61.

8 *Chart. St Mary's Abbey*, ii. 390; Simpson, *A Treatise*, 148; Levett, *Studies in Manorial History*, Table 2.

9 Hirst, *Conquest of Plague*, 33-5, 222; Biraben, *La peste*, i. 12; Zinnser, *Rats, Lice and History*, 50ff.; Shrewsbury, *History*, 5; Crawfurd, *Plague*, 120; Simpson, *A Treatise*, 260ff.

10 Manchester, 'The palaeopathology of urban infections', 13.

11 See Morris, 'The plague in Britain', 205-24; McNeill, *Plagues*, 168; Shrewsbury, *History*, 6ff; Twigg, *Black Death*, 113ff.

12 Clyn, *Annals*, 36; Horrox, 69, 62; Knighton, *Chronicle*, 97; Gwynn, 'The Black Death', 34; Barnes, *History*, 440; see Horrox, 178 and note 25.

13 *Chart. St Mary's Abbey*, i. 378-82, ii.37-40; *Reg. Hospital of St John the Baptist*, xx-xxi.

14 *Annals*, 37; *Materials for the history of the Franciscan Province*, 141; Moorman, *History*, 351 n.6.

15 *Reg. de Kilmainham*, xii; see also Gwynn, 'The Black Death in Ireland', 39-41; Walsh, *Richard FitzRalph*, 266-8.

16 *C.P.L*, iii. 290, 536; C.P.P., i. 259, 287, 412; *Fasti of St Patrick's Cathedral*, 68, 60, 69, 150ff; *Reg. de Kilmainham*, xii; Gwynn & Hadcock, *Medieval Religious Houses*, 74; 'Cal. Christ Church Deeds', No. 240, p.81.

17 Shrewsbury, *History*, 55; Hatcher, *Plague*, 26; Ziegler, *The Black Death*, 235-6; Russell, *British Medieval Population*, 222; Dohar, *The Black Death and Pastoral Leadership*, 41.

18 Gwynn, 'The Black Death', 37-8; Gwynn & Hadcock, *Medieval Religious Houses*, 4.

19 Horrox, 170, 53-4; Meinsma, *De Zwarte Dood*, 302-3.

20 Mollat, *Les pauvres au Moyen Âge*, 236; Heuser (ed.), *Die Kildare-Gedichte*, 81-5, 133-9, 154-8; *Decameron*, 56.

21 Richardson & Sayles, *Administration of Ireland*, 88; Cosgrove, 'Chief Governors of Ireland', 473; Burke, *History of the Lord Chancellors*, 13; Wood, 'The office of Chief Governor of Ireland'; Gwynn, 'The Black Death in Ireland', 38-41; *Chart. St Mary's Abbey*, ii. 391.

22 Richardson & Sayles, *Administration of Ireland*, 95-6, 102, 106-112; 28; Brand, 'Chancellors and Keepers of the Great Seal', 500-508.

23 Berry, 'Catalogue of mayors', 153-62; Hill, 'Mayors and Lord Mayors of Dublin', 549-50; *Chart. St Mary's Abbey*, ii. 391; D'Alton, *History of County Dublin*, 47.

24 *Cal. Pat. Rolls 1354-8*, p. 91; *C.P.L*, iii. 432.

25 Livi-Bacci, *A Concise History of World Population*, 49; Bowsky, 'The impact of the Black Death', 1-34; Horrox, 34 -5; Pounds, *An Economic History of Medieval Europe*, 153-4; Knighton, *Chronicle*, 97; Biraben, *La peste*, i. 157-61; Hollingsworth, *Historical Demography*, 362-4, 368-9.

26 Cited Gwynn, 'The Black Death', 32; Creighton, *A History of Epidemics*, i. 131.

27 Shrewsbury, *History*, 49; Clarke, '*Urbs et suburbium*', 45-58.

28 Hollingsworth, *Historical Demography*, 269; Hatcher, *Plague*, 29; Ziegler, *The Black Death*, 235-9; Platt, *King Death*, 9; Horrox, 3; Razi, *Medieval Parish*, 103.

29 Nicholas, *Medieval Flanders*, 266; Gottfried, 'The Black Death', 261; Postan, 'Some economic evidence of declining population', 130-67; Hatcher, *Plague*, 36; Hollingsworth, *Historical Demography*, 385; Livi-Bacci, *A Concise History*, 31, 53; *Roll of Proceedings of King's Council*, 138-9

30 *Parl. and Councils of Medieval Ireland*, No. xvi.

31 Mac Niocaill, 'Socio-economic problems of the medieval town', 18-19; Hatcher, 'Mortality in the fifteenth century', 29 and *Plague*, 63.

32 Mac Niocaill, 'Socio-economic problems', 18-19; Houston, *Population History*, 122; Hollingsworth, *Historical Demography*, 385; Hatcher, *Plague*, 61-73.

3:RESPONSES TO THE PLAGUE

1 Whelan, 'The famine and post-famine adjustment', 157.

2 Carpentier, *'Autour de la peste noire'*, 1084.

3 Clyn, *Annals*, 37, trans. Horrox, 83.

4 Binski, *Medieval Death*, 129; see Harper-Bill, 'The English Church and English religion after the Black Death'.

5 Knighton, *Chronicle*, 97; *Piers the Ploughman*, passus V, line 13; C.P.P., i. 287; see Kelly, *A History of the Black Death in Ireland*, 58-60.

6 Cal Pat. Rolls, 1348-50, p. 197; Gilbert, *A History of the City of Dublin*, i.

324-5, 418-420; *Chart. St Mary's Abbey*, i. 16-21; see O'Sullivan, 'The Dominicans in medieval Dublin', 95-6.

7 Wallace, 'The archaeology of Anglo-Norman Dublin', 404 and 'Anglo-Norman Dublin', 260-261.

8 *C.P.L.*, iii. 311, 396, 335; Mac Leod, 'Some late medieval wood sculptures', 54-5; *AFM*, v. 1448n.

9 *Annals*, 35.

10 Keen, *English Society*, 35; Lydon, *Lordship*, 114-5.

11 Dols, *The Black Death in the Middle East*, 240 n.40, 294, 298-301.

12 C.P.L., iii. 311; Walsh, *FitzRalph*, 340 n.71; Horrox, 44, 60.

13 Colledge (ed.), *Poems of Richard Ledrede*, 71-3; 137.

14 Horrox, 193-4.

15 Nutton, 'The Seeds of Disease', 1-34; Arrizabalaga, 'Facing the Black Death', 275; *Decameron*, 51-2.

16 Arrizabalaga, Facing the Black Death, 274; Horrox, 175.

17 Lydgate, 'A Doctrine for Pestilence', ll.1-3, cited Wenzel, 'Pestilence', 150; see Nohl, *The Black Death*, 230-240.

18 *Hist. & Mun. Docs. Ire.*, 234, 257. On leprosy, see Porter, *The Greatest Benefit to Mankind*, 121-2, 126; Rawcliffe, *Medicine and Society*, 14-17; on leprosy in Ireland, see Creighton, *A History of Epidemics*, i.100; Fleetwood, *History of Medicine in Ireland*, 12-13, 30; Robins, *Miasma*, 11-12; on hospitals in Dublin, see Gwynn and Hadcock, *Medieval Religious Houses*, 344ff.

19 Gilbert, *History of Dublin*, i. Appendix viii, pp. 426-8; Shaw, 'Medieval medico-philosophical treaties', 144ff. and 'Medicine in Ireland'; McGrath, *Education in Ancient and Medieval Ireland*, 211; cited Dunlevy, 'The medical families of medieval Ireland', 19-20.

20 See Heuser, (ed.), *Die Kildare-Gedichte*, 81-5, 133-9; *Cal. Pat. Rolls, 1330-1334*, p. 552; *C.P.L.*, iii. 590; see also Hennessy, 'The Priory and Hospital of New Gate', 48ff; McNeill, C., 'Hospital of St John', 77-82.

21 Bliss, *The inscribed slates at Smarmore*, 33-60; Mac Giolla Phádraig, 'Fourteenth-century life in a Dublin monastery', 121; Tommaso del Garbo, *Consilio contro alla peste*, cited Henderson, 'The Black Death in Florence', 138ff; Bliss and Long, 'Literature in Norman French and English', 735. On medical responses to plague in general, see Arrizabalaga, 'Facing the Black Death', 284-5.

22 Horrox, 194, 191; Simpson, *A Treatise*, 317-8; see Nohl, *The Black Death*, 87ff for a full description of these sorts of remedies.

23 Meinsma, *De Zwarte Dood*, 300-30; J-J.de Smet (ed.), *Recueil des Chroniques de Flandre* 11, 380-382; Boccaccio, *Decameron*, 50; Horrox, 52-3, 194-203; Henderson, 'The Black Death in Florence', 141-5.

24 *CARD*, i. 236.

25 Park, 'Medicine and the Renaissance, 66-79; Simpson, *A Treatise*, 336ff.; *CARD*, ii. 139.

26 Thompson, 'The aftermath of the Black Death and the aftermath of the Great War', 565-72.

27 Horrox, 30, 85; di Tura in Bowsky (ed.), *The Black Death*, 14; *Cronica Fiorentina di Marchionne di Coppo Stefani*; www.temple-bar.ie/history; www.excavations.ie (Nos. 78, 092); Brady, K. and Kelleher, C., 'Swords, plague and pestilence', 8-11.

28 See, for example, the accounts in Nohl, *The Black Death*, 164ff.

29 *C.P.L.*, iii. 606; *C.P.L.*, iv. 106; Colledge (ed.), *Poems of Richard Ledrede*, No. XXXVII, p. 91; Heuser (ed.), *Die Kildare-Gedichte*, 133-9, 154-8; Jean de Venette in Horrox, 57.

30 *Cronica Fiorentina di Marchionne di Coppo Stefani* ; cited Meiss, *Painting in Florence and Siena*, 67.

31 Walsh, *FitzRalph*, 282-8, 314, 320, 323-5, 337, 343-7; Gwynn, 'Richard FitzRalph', vi, 86; Horrox, 57.

32 *C.P.L.*,iv. 87, 12; Mollat, *Les Pauvres au Moyen Âge*, 135, 231-2; Dyer, *Standards of Living*, 238; Cullum, 'Poverty and charity in early four-teenth-century England', 140-41, 149-51.

33 *Piers the Ploughman*, Prologue, ll. 81-4, p. 27; Gwynn, 'Richard FitzRalph', vi. 84, 85ff and 'Archbishop FitzRalph and George of Hungary', 562-3; Walsh, FitzRalph, 329-331, 337; C.P.L., 1431-1447, p. 227.

34 Cited Watt, *The Church in Medieval Ireland*, 182; Heuser (ed.), *Die Kildare-Gedichte*, 155-6; Seymour, *Anglo-Irish Literature*, 111, 113.

35 Watt, *The Church in Medieval Ireland*, 193; *Materials for the History of the Franciscan Province*, 158-9, 225; Moorman, *History*, 341ff; Horrox, 75.

36 Owst, *Literature and Pulpit in Medieval England*, 533; Huizinga, *The Waning of the Middle Ages*, p. 134; Binski, *Medieval Death*, 163; see also 128.

37 See Hourihane, '"Holye Crossys"' 1-85.

38 Cohn, 'The place of the dead', 29, 26ff; cited Lydon, 'The medieval city', 36-7.

39 Hunt, *Irish Medieval Figure Sculpture*, i. 57,105-7, 114-6, 214; ii. Plates 140-41 (tombs at St Audoen's), Plates 192-3 (St Lawrence Tomb in St Mary's Abbey, Howth) and Plates 145, 204-7 (tombs in St Werburgh's). See Cohn, 'The place of the dead'; Horrox, 245 and note 36; Platt, *King Death*, 139ff.

40 Rae, 'Architecture and sculpture', 760-1, 774.

41 Hourihane, 'Holye Crossys', 33.

42 See Hunt, *Irish Medieval Figure Sculpture*, i. 53ff; Duby, *The Age of Cathedrals* 195-220.

43 See Mc Neill, 'Church building in fourteenth-century Ireland'; Hunt, *Irish Medieval Figure Sculpture*, i., 114; Stalley, 'Irish Gothic and English fashion', 79 and 'Gothic art and architecture', 172ff.

4: LONG-TERM EFFECTS

1 Trevalyan, *English Social History*, xi; Pounds, *An Economic History of Medieval Europe*, 440–1; Gasquet, *The Great Pestilence*, xvi; Hecker, *The Black Death*, preface; xi; Gottfried, The Black Death, 266.

2 Excerpts from the Plea Rolls, MS 193; CARD, i. 139; Richardson & Sayles, *Irish Parliament*, 239; Cosgrove, 'Parliaments in Ireland', 593–608.

3 Connolly, 'Pleas held before the Chief Governors', 120-126.

4 *Cal. Close Rolls* 1349–54, p. 292.

5 *Statutes of the Realm* in Horrox, 287–9.

6 *Chart. St Mary's Abbey*, ii. xiv-xv.

7 *Piers the Ploughman*, Prologue, ll. 40-45, p. 26; cited Jusserand, *English Wayfaring Life*, 149; Miller, 'The economic policies of governments', 321.

8 CARD, ii. 132-5, iii, No.11; iv., 235. *Statutes, John-Henry V*, 374-396.

9 CP., i. 19, 119, 462, 467, passim; Gwynn, 'The medieval university of St Patrick's Dublin', 199ff, and 'Anglo-Irish church life', 30; Knighton, *Chronicle*, 103.

10 Horrox, 57; Gwynn, 'Richard FitzRalph', 399; CPP, i. 467.

11 *C.P.L.*, iii. 354; *C.P.P.*, i. 193.

12 Moorman, *History*, 344, 351-2; *C.P.L.*, iii. 283.

13 *CPP*, i. 469; *C.P.L.*, iii. 432; *C.P.L.*, iv. 12; Connolly, 'Irish material in the class of Ancient Petitions', SC8/93/4601, p.32; *C.P.L.*, iii. 384, 430; *Reg. Swayne*, 1-2.

14 *C.P.L.*, iii. 361, 426, 427; *Fasti of St Patrick's Cathedral*, 163; Bernard, 'Richard Talbot', 225; *Dignitas Decani*, 104-6.

15 *Hist and Mun. Docs.*, 227, 362-4.

16 *Cal. Close Rolls*, 1369-74, p. 420; Clarke, M.V., 'William of Windsor in Ireland' 191.

17 Keen, *English Society*, 93-4; Hibbert, 'The economic policies of towns', 200, 205, 211; Mac Niocaill, 'Socio-economic problems' 10, 11, 14-15, 21.

18 Pounds, *An Economic History of Medieval Europe*, 456, 448ff; Mollat, *Les pauvres au Moyen Âge*, 294ff; Harper-Bill, 'The English church and English religion', 116.

19 *C.P.L*, iii. 606; *Cal. Close Rolls*, 1405-9, p. 178; cited Cosgrave, 'The emergence of the Pale', 542.

20 Pounds, *An Economic History of Medieval Europe*, 440-441.

21 *Cal. Justic. Rolls*, 1305-7, ii. 6; *Cal. Archbishop Alen's Register*, 171; Mills, 'Tenants and agriculture', 56 and 'Notices of the manor of St Sepulchre', 37-41; *Cal. Pat. Rolls*, 1330-34, p. 551.

22 *Cal. of liber niger and liber albus*, 43-5; see Sayles, 'Legal proceedings', 45.

23 *Cal. Pat. Rolls*, 1350-54, p. 253; *CARD*, i. Nos. 37, 40, 42, 53, 59, 60, and *passim*; *Cal Pat. Rolls*, *1354-8*, p. 91.

24 Otway-Ruthven, 'The medieval church lands of County Dublin', 54-72;

Chart. St Mary's Abbey, i. 275; *Cal. Pat. Rolls*, 1330-34, p. 552; *Reg. Swayne*, 4-5; see Hennessy, 'The priory and hospital of New Gate', 49-50.

25 *C.P.L.*, ii. 27; *Cal. Doc. Ire. 1302-7*, pp. 237-44.

26 *C.P.L.*, iii. 432; *'Cal of liber albus and liber niger,'* Nos. 6, 61; Reg. All Hallows, 78; 'Cal. of register of Archbishop Fleming', No. 133; *Dignitas Decani*, No. 130, p.139; *C.P.L.*, v. 303, 325.

27 Hennessy, 'The priory and hospital of New Gate', 49-50; *C.P.L.*, v. 303; McNeill , C., 'The hospital of St John without the New Gate Dublin', 62-4.

28 *Chronicle*, 105; Gen. Office MS 192; Chancery Miscellanea, C.47/10/22 (2) m.2; Walsh, C., *Archaeological excavations at Patrick, Nicholas and Winetavern Streets, Dublin*, 121.

29 *C.P.L*, iv. 163, 506; *Cal. Pat. Rolls, 1370-4*, p. 302.

30 *CARD*, i. 30.

31 *C.P.L.*, iii. 432; *Cal. Pat. Rolls, 1354-8*, p. 91; P.R.O.I., R.C.8/28, 157-8, 679-80; see Lyons, 'Weather', 46.

32 *Cal. Pat. Rolls, 1350-54*, pp. 253, 235, 415; Gransden, *Historical Writing*, ii. 172-3; *CARD*, i. 172-3, 235, 275, 278, 284-5, 287, 293, 300, 308, 310-11, 320, 336, 337, 343, 346-7; Cosgrove, 'The emergence of the Pale', 551-2.

33 Childs and O'Neill, 'Overseas trade', 501-2, 511, 515ff; *P.R.I. Rep. D. K.*, No. 39, pp. 34-5; No. 38, pp. 30, 43, 55, 63, 85; No. 36, p. 28; No. 37, pp. 24, 25, 38, 48; No. 54, pp. 40-43.

34 Beresford, *New Towns of the Middle Ages*; Du Boulay, *An Age of Ambition*, 45.

35 *Textes et documents d'histoire du Moyen Âge*, xxx-xxxi; Pounds, *Historical Geography*, 339-40; Rorig, *The Medieval Town*, 115.

36 *Cal. Close Rolls, 1360-64*, p. 131; *Cal. Close Rolls, 1354-60*, pp. 575-6.

37 *CELT; CARD*, ii. 132-5, iii. No. 11, iv. 235; *Statutes, John-Henry V*, 374-396.

38 *Statutes of the Realm II*, in Horrox, 323-6.

39 *Cal. Close Rolls, 1354-60*, pp. 587, 575; *Stat. Ire., John-Henry V*, pp. 568-9; see Cosgrave, *Late Medieval Ireland*, 18-20, 33-6.

40 *Facsimiles of National Mss of Ireland*. III, xxxix; *CARD*, i. 322; Cosgrave, 'England and Ireland 1399-1447', pp. 529-30; *Cal. Pat. Rolls, 1413-16*, p.122.

41 *CARD*, i. 30; cited Green, *The Making of Ireland*, 131-2; Gilbert, *Viceroys of Ireland*, 331.

42 Frame, 'Two Kings in Leinster', 165 and *passim*; Lydon, 'Medieval Wicklow', 175-7.

43 *Parliaments and Councils*, i. 19-22; *Cal. Fine Rolls*, 1356-68, p. 308; see Frame, *English Lordship in Ireland*, 315-7 .

44 cited Cosgrave, 'The emergence of the Pale', 533

45 *Chart. St Mary's Abbey*, ii. p. xix.

5: AFTER 1348

1 Horrox, 83.

2 Hatcher, *Plague*, 63ff; Simpson, *A Treatise*, 159-61; Slack, *The Impact of Plague in Tudor and Stuart England*, 144-72; Bolton, 'The world upside down', 27; Gottfried, *Epidemic Disease in Fifteenth-Century England*.

3 Keeling and Gilligan, 'Metapopulation dynamics of bubonic plague', 903-6; Shrewsbury, *History*, 156; Langland, *Piers the Ploughman*, Passus xx, ll. 80-4, 97-8, pp. 247-8; see Manchester and Roberts, *The Archaeology of Disease*.

4 Pye, G., *A Discourse of the plague; wherein Dr Mead's notions are consider'd and refuted* (1721), cited Twigg, 'Plague in London', 12.

5 Herlihy and Klapisch-Zumer, *Tuscans and their Families*, 73-8.

6 *Chart. St Mary's Abbey*, ii. 395; *ALC*, 23; *AFM*, iii. 621; Porter, *The Greatest Benefit to Mankind*, 282; *P.R.O.I.*, Mem. Rolls, R.C.8/28, 157-8; *Chronicle*, 185; Horrox, 85-7.

7 *Chart. St Mary's Abbey*, ii. 397, also 282.

8 Watts, *Epidemics*, 1; Hollingsworth, 'Plague mortality rates by age and sex'; Russell, *British Medieval Population*, 230-1, 260-70 and 'Late ancient and medieval populations', 31; Hatcher, *Plague*, 62-68; Pounds, *An Economic History of Medieval Europe*, 139.

9 Horrox, 89; Clyn, *Annals*, 38; AFM, iv. 691; *Ann. Clon.*, 308; Harris, *History and Antiquities of the City of Dublin*, Chap. XI.

10 Horrox, 91; Clyn, *Annals*, 38; *Roll of Proceedings of Kings's Council*, 138-40; *A.F.M.*, iv. 763, 765.

11 *AFM*, iv. 801, 841, 861, 863, 911, 953; *A.U.*, iii. 97, 117; *A.L.C.*ii. 97, 117, 125, 153, 159; Harris, *History and Antiquities*, Chap. XI.

12 *A.F.M.*, iv. 865, 917, 952.

13 *A.F.M.*, iv. 962, 984, 1029, 1049, 1055, 1107, 1135, 1157, 1247 1107; Harris, *History and Antiquities*, Chap. X.

14 *AFM*, iv. 1045, 1167, 1175; *CARD*, i. 139.

15 *CARD*, i. 236, 300-1; see Park, *Medicine and the Renaissance*, 66-79.

16 Pounds, *An Economic History of Medieval Europe*, 446-7.

17 Logan, 'Pestilence in the Irish wars', 279-90; *AFM*, v. 1349; *ALC*, ii. 229; *SPD*, 11.iii. 38-9.

18 Harris, *History and Antiquities*, Chap. XI (a); Creighton, *History of Epidemics*, i. 371-3; AU. iii. 604.

19 Camden, W., *Britannia*, cited Butlin, 'Land and people', 158.

20 *AFM*, v. 1681; *Annals of Ireland by Friar Clyn and Thady Dowling*, 41.

21 *CARD*, i.139; ii.100-102, 103-4; ii. 63; O'Meara,' The kingdom of Dalkey'.

22 *CARD*, ii. 419-20, 424; iii. 536-8; Dekker, 'A Rod for Run-awayes', 147ff; MacGiolla Phádraig, 'Speed's Plan of Dublin', ii. 102; Simpson,

A Treatise, 343-5.

23 Corish, 'The Cromwellian conquest', 345ff.; Shrewsbury, *History*, 433; cited Creighton, *A History of Epidemics*, i. 566.

24 *CARD*, iv, 1-4, 10, 501-2; Gilbert, *History of the City of Dublin*, i. 165.

25 See Doolin, *Dublin's Medical Schools*, 5; 3; Kelly, J., 'The emergence of scientific and institutional medical practice', 23ff.; Millett, 'Irish literature in Latin', 566; cited Robins, *Miasma*, 10; Crawford, 'Typhus in nineteenth-century Ireland', 129-32.

26 Dekker, 'A Rod for Run-awayes', 141; Robin, *Miasma*, 21-4; *CARD*, iii. 118-9.

27 *CARD*, ii.196; see Moylan, 'Vagabonds and sturdy beggars', 193ff.

28 *A Bibliography of the Royal Proclamations of the Tudor and Stuart Sovereigns*, cited Shrewsbury, *History*, 434.

29 Clarke, 'The Irish economy 1600-60', pp. 168-86; Dickson, 'Capital and country: 1600-1800', pp. 63-76; Andrews, 'Land and people, c.1685', pp. 476-7; Simms, J.G.,' The Restoration', 448; Cullen, 'Economic trends 1660-1691', pp. 388-9 and 'The growth of Dublin', 251 and note 2, p.277.

30 Craddock, *City of Plagues*, 130ff, 147-60; see Aalen, 'Health and housing in Dublin c.1850-1921', pp. 279-304; Robins, *Miasma*, 229ff.

31 McNeill, *Plagues and Peoples*, 159, 326; Bewley, 'An account of the Biological Club'.

32 Zinsser, *Rats, Lice and History*, 69; Simpson, *A Treatise*, 33, 350; on the use of stone in Dublin, see Prunty, 'Improving the urban environment', 166ff .

33 McNeill, *Plagues*, 170; Zinsser, *Rats, Lice and History*, 43; Livi-Bacci, *A Concise History*, 54; Biraben, *La peste*, i. 17-20.

34 WHO, *Epidemiology, Distribution, Surveillance and Control*, 15; Inglesby, et al., 'Plague as a biological weapon', 2281-2290; www.cdc.gov /plague (Center for Disease Control, USA); http://www.hopkins-iodefense.org/pages/agents/agentplague.html

35 www.cdc.gov/ plague (Center for Disease Control, USA); *New England Journal of Medicine*, Vol. 337, No. 10 (1997), 667-80.

36 Parkhill, *et al.*, 'Genome sequence of *Yersinia pestis*, the causative agent of plague', 523-7.

Bibliography

MANUSCRIPT SOURCES

Public Record Office London: Chancery Miscellanea: C 47/10/22.
Public Record Office Ireland: Memoranda Rolls, 35-39; Edward III, RC
    8/28.
Genealogical Office, Dublin: Excerpts from the Plea Rolls, MS 192-194.

PRIMARY PRINTED SOURCES

Account Roll of the Priory of the Holy Trinity, Dublin 1337-1346, ed. Mills, J.
    (1891, reprinted Dublin, 1996).
Annals of Christ Church Dublin, ed. Gwynn, A., Anal. Hib., 16 (1946), 324-
    9.
Annals of Clonmacnoise, ed. Murphy, D. (Dublin, 1896).
Annals of Connacht AD 1224-1544, ed. Freeman, A.M. (Dublin, 1944).
Annals of Innisfallen, ed. Mac Airt, S. (Dublin, 1951).
Annals of Ireland (Annales Hiberniae) by Friar John Clyn and Thady Dowling,
    Chancellor of Leighlin, ed. Butler, R. (Dublin, 1849).
'Annals of Ireland from the year 1443 to 1468, translated from the Irish by
    Dudley MacFirbis, for Sir James Ware in the year 1666', in *Annals of the
    Kingdom of Ireland by the Four Masters*, ed. O'Donovan, J.Vol. iv. (Dublin,
    1848).
*Annals of the Kingdom of Ireland by the Four Masters, from the Earliest Period
    to the Year 1616*, ed. O'Donovan, J., 7 vols. (Dublin, 1848-51).
Annals of Loch Cé: A Chronicle of Irish Affairs, 1014-1590, ed. Hennessy,
    W.H., 2 vols. (London, 1871).
'Annals of Nenagh', ed. Gleeson, D., *Anal. Hib.*, 12 (1943), 155-164.

'Annals of St Mary's Abbey, Dublin' and 'Annals of Ireland' in *Chartularies of St Mary's Abbey, Dublin*, Vol. 2 (London 1884), 241-399.

Annals of Ulster, 431-1541, ed. Hennessy, W.M. and MacCarthy, B., 4 vols. (Dublin, 1887-1901).

Black Book of Christ Church, ed. Gwynn, A., Anal. Hib., 16 (1946), 281-337.

Boccaccio, G., *Decameron*, trans. McWilliam, G.H. (Penguin, Harmondsworth, 1972).

Calendar of the Ancient Records of Dublin, ed. Gilbert, J.T., 19 vols. (Dublin, 1889-1944).

Calendar of Archbishop Alen's Register, c.1172-1534, ed. McNeill, C. (Dublin, 1950).

Calendar of Christ Church Deeds, in Reports of the Deputy Keeper of the Public Records of Ireland, Nos. 20, 23, 24 (1888-9, 1891-2).

Calendar of Close Rolls, 1272-1500, 45 vols., ed. Tresham (London, 1892-1963).

Calendar of Documents Relating to Ireland, 1171-1307, ed. Sweetman, H.S., 5 vols. (London, 1875-86).

Calendar of Entries in the Papal Registers Relating to Great Britain and Ireland, Papal Letters, Vols.I-XIV (1198-1492), ed. Bliss, Johnson, Twemlow (London, 1897-1960).

Calendar of Entries in the Papal Registers relating to Great Britain and Ireland. Petitions to the Pope, i. 1342-1491, ed. Bliss (London, 1896).

Calendar of Fine Rolls (London, 1911-).

Calendar of the Justiciary Rolls, Ireland, 1305-7, ed. Mills, J. (Dublin, 1914).

'Calendar of the liber niger and liber albus of Christ Church, Dublin', ed. Lawlor, H.J., PRIA., 27C (1908-9), 1-93.

Calendar of Patent Rolls (London, 1891-1971).

'Calendar of the Register of Archbishop Fleming', ed. Lawlor, H.J., PRIA, 30C (1912), 94-190.

Calendar of State Papers and Letters Domestic series, 2 vols., ed. Brewer, J.S. (London, 1830-34).

Chartularies of St Mary's Abbey Dublin and Annals of Ireland, 1162-1370, ed. Gilbert, J.T., 2 vols. (London, 1884-6, 1965).

'Chronicle of Pembridge', in *Black Book of Christ Church*, ed. Gwynn, Anal. Hib., 16 (March 1946).

Cronica Fiorentina di Marchionne di Coppo Stefani, ed. Rodolico, N. (Citta di Castello, 1903-13), http://jefferson.village.virginia.edu/osheim/marchione.htm

CELT: Corpus of Electronic Texts Online, University College Cork: www.ucc.ie/celt

Dignitas Decani of St Patrick's Cathedral, Dublin, ed. White, N.B. (Dublin 1957).

Erasmus: Correspondence of Erasmus, Letters 1523-4, trans. Mynors, R. and Dalzell, A. (Toronto, 1992).

Bibliography

Facsimiles of National Mss of Ireland, ed. Gilbert, J. (London, 1874-84).

Fasti of St Patrick's Cathedral, Dublin, ed. Lawlor, H.J. (Dublin, 1930).

Froissart's Chronicles, ed. and trans. Jolliffe, J. (London 1967).

Historic and Municipal Documents of Ireland, 1172-1320, from the Archives of the City of Dublin, ed. Gilbert, J.T. (London, 1870).

'Kilkenny Chronicle in Cotton MS Vespasian B.XI', ed. Flower, R., Anal. Hib. 2 (1931).

Knighton, *Chronicle 1337-1396*, ed. and trans. G. H. Martin (Oxford 1995).

Irish Historical Documents 1172-1922, ed. Curtis, E. and McDowell, R.B. (London, 1943).

Langland, William, *The Vision of William concerning Piers the Ploughman*, ed. Skeat, W.W. (Oxford, 1886), trans. Goodridge, J.F. (Penguin: Harmondsworth, 1970.

Liber Primus Kilkenniensis, ed. McNeill, C. (Dublin 1931); trans. Otway-Ruthven, A.J. (Kilkenny, 1961).

Materials for the History of the Franciscan Province of Ireland 1230-1450, ed. Fitzmaurice, E.B. and Little, A.G (Manchester, 1920).

Parliaments and Councils of Medieval Ireland, ed. Richardson, H.G. and Sayles, G.O. (Dublin, 1947).

Registers of Christ Church Cathedral, Dublin, ed. Refaussé, R. and Lennon, C. (Dublin 1998).

Register of the Hospital of St John the Baptist without the Newgate, Dublin, ed. Brooks, E. St John (Dublin, 1936).

Registrum de Kilmainham: Register of Chapter Acts of the Hospital of St John of Jerusalem in Ireland, 1326-1339, ed. McNeill, C. (Dublin, 1932).

Register of John Swayne, Archbishop of Armagh and Primate of Ireland, 1418-39, ed. Chart, D.A. (Belfast,

Registrum Prioratus Omnium Sanctorum juxta Dublin, ed. Butler, R. (Dublin, 1935).

Roll of the Proceedings of the King's Council in Ireland, ed. Graves, J. (London, 1877).

Statutes and Ordinances and Acts of the Parliament of Ireland: King John to Henry V, ed. Berry, H.F. (Dublin, 1907).

Statute Rolls, Ireland: Henry VI, ed. Berry, H.F. (Dublin, 1910).

Textes et documents d'histoire du Moyen Âge, XIVe – XV siècles, ed. Glénisson J. and Day, J. (Paris 1970).

SECONDARY SOURCES

Aalen, F.H., *Man and the Landscape in Ireland* (London, 1978).
–, and Whelan, K. (ed.), *Dublin City and County: From Prehistory to Present* (Dublin, 1992).
–, 'Health and housing in Dublin c.1850-1921', in Aalen and Whelan (ed.), *Dublin: From Prehistory to Present* (Dublin, 1992), 279-304.
Andrews, J. H., 'The oldest map of Dublin', PRIA, 83C (1983), 205-37.
–, 'Land and people c.1685', NHI, iii, 454-77.
Arrizabalaga, J., 'Facing the Black Death: perceptions and reactions of university medical practitioners' in Garcia-Ballester, *et al.* (ed.), *Practical Medicine from Salerno to the Black Death* (Cambridge, 1994), 237-288.
–, *et al.* (eds.), *Medicine from the Black Death to the French Disease* (Aldershot, 1998).
Bailey, M., 'Demographic decline in late medieval England: some thoughts on recent research', *Economic History Review*, 49 (1996) 1-19.
–, '"*Per impetum maris*": natural disaster and economic decline in eastern England, 1275-1350' in Campbell, B. (ed.), *Before the Black Death: Studies in the Crisis of the Early Fourteenth Century* (Manchester & New York, 1991), 184-208.
Ball, F.E., *History of County Dublin* (Dublin, 1906; reprinted 1995).
Bardon, J. and Conlin, S., *Dublin: One Thousand Years of Wood Quay* (Belfast, 1984).
Barnes, J., *The History of that Most Victorious Monarch, Edward III* (Cambridge, 1688).
Barry, T.B., *The Archaeology of Medieval Ireland* (London, 1987).
–, and Frame, R. and Simms, K. (eds.), *Colony and Frontier in Medieval Ireland* (London, 1995).
Bassett, S. (ed.), *Death in Towns: Urban Responses to the Dying and the Dead, 100-1600* (London and New York, 1995).
Bean, J.M.W., 'Plague, population and economic decline in England in the later Middle Ages', *Economic History Review*, 2nd series, XV (1962-3), 422-37.
Bede, *Ecclesiastical History of the English People*, ed. Colgrave, B. and Mynors, R. (Oxford, 1969).
Beresford, M.W., *New Towns of the Middle Ages* (London, 1967).
Bernard, J.H., 'Richard Talbot, Archbishop and Chancellor, 1418-49', PRIA, 35C (1918), 218-29.
Berry, H.F., 'Catalogue of the mayors, provosts and bailiffs of Dublin city, A.D. 1229 to 1447' in PRIA, 28C (1910), 47-61, reprinted with corrections in Clarke (ed.), *Medieval Dublin: The Living City* (Dublin, 1990), 153-62.
Bewley, G., 'An account of the Biological Club', *Irish Journal of Medical Science*, series 6 (1960).

Binski, P., *Medieval Death: Ritual and Representation* (London, 1996).

Biraben, J.N., *Les hommes et la peste en France en dans les pays européens et méditerranéens,* 2 vols. (Paris, 1975).

Bliss, A.J., 'The inscribed slates at Smarmore' PRIA, 64C, No. 2 (1965-6), 33-60.

—, 'Language and literature', in Lydon (ed.), *The English in Medieval Ireland: Proceedings of the First Joint Meeting of the Royal Irish Academy and the British Academy, Dublin 1982,* (Dublin, 1984), 27-45.

—, and Long, J., 'Literature in Norman French and English to 1534' in NHI ii. 708-36.

Bolton, J., 'The world upside down: Plague as an agent of economic and social change' in Ormrod and Lindley (eds.), *The Black Death in England* (Stamford, 1996).

—, 'Irish migration to England in the later Middle Ages: the evidence of 1394 and 1440', IHS, 32, No. 125 (2000), 1-21.

Bowsky, W.J., 'The impact of the Black Death upon Sienese government and society,' *Speculum,* 39, i (January 1964), 1-34.

—, (ed.), *The Black Death: A Turning Point in History?* (New York, 1971).

Brady, J., and Simms, A. (ed.), *Dublin Through Space and Time, c.900-1900* (Dublin, 2000).

Brady, K. and Kelleher, C., 'Swords, plague and pestilence', *Archaeology Ireland* (Autumn 2000), 8-11.

Brand, P., 'Chancellors and Keepers of the Great Seal, 1232-1534', in Moody, Martin, Byrne (eds.), *A New History of Ireland,* ix (Oxford, 1984), 500-508.

Britnell, R. and Hatcher, J., *Progress and Problems in Medieval England* (Cambridge, 1996).

Burke, O., *The History of the Lord Chancellors of Ireland, 1186-1874* (Dublin, 1879).

Butler, W.F.T., 'Town life in medieval Ireland', *Journal Cork Historical and Archaeological Society,* 8, 2nd series (1901).

Butlin, R.A. (ed.), *The Development of the Irish Town* (London, 1977).

—, 'Irish towns in the sixteenth and seventeenth centuries' in Butlin (ed.), *The Development of the Irish Town,* 61-100.

—, 'The population of Dublin in the late seventeenth century', *Irish Geography,* v, 2 (1965), 51-66.

—, 'Land and people, c.1600' in NHI, iii., 142-67.

Campbell, B., (ed.), *Before the Black Death: Studies in the 'Crisis' of the Early Fourteenth Century* (Manchester, 1991).

—, 'Population pressure, inheritance and the land market in a fourteenth-century peasant community' in Smith, R.M. (ed.), *Land, Kinship and Life-Cycle* (Cambridge, 1984), 87-134.

Cantwell, I., 'Anthropozoological relationships in late medieval Dublin', *Dublin Historical Review,* LIV, No. 1 (Spring 2001), 73-80.

Carmichael, A., *Plague and the Poor in Renaissance Florence* (Cambridge, 1986).

Carpentier, E., '*Autour de la peste noire: famine et épidémies dans l'histoire du XIVième siècle*', *Annales (Economies, Sociétés, Civilisation.)*, 17, 6 (November-December 1962), 1062-92.

Childs, W. and O'Neill, T., 'Overseas trade' in NHI, ii. 492-524.

Cipolla, *Fighting the Plague in Seventeenth-Century Italy* (Wisconsin, 1981).

Clarke, A., 'The Irish economy, 1600-1660' in NHI, iii. 168-86.

Clarke, H.B., *Dublin c.840 to c.1540: The Medieval Town in the Modern City* (Dublin, 1978).

— (ed.), *Medieval Dublin: The Making of a Metropolis* (Dublin, 1990).

—(ed.), *Medieval Dublin: The Living City* (Dublin, 1990).

—, 'The mapping of medieval Dublin: A case study in thematic cartography' in Clarke, H.B. and Simms, A. (eds.), *A Comparative History of Urban Origins* (Oxford, 1985), 617-43.

— , 'The topographical development of early medieval Dublin' in JRSAI, 107 (1977), 29-51, reprinted Clarke, (ed.), *Medieval Dublin: The Making of a Metropolis* (Dublin, 1990), 52-69.

— and Simms, A. (ed.), *The Comparative History of Urban Origins in Non-Roman Europe: Ireland, Wales, Denmark, Germany, Poland and Russia from the Ninth to the Thirteenth Century* (Oxford, 1985).

— and Simms, A., 'Towards a comparative history of urban origins' in Clarke, H.B., and Simms, A., (eds.), *The Comparative History of Urban Origins in non-Roman Europe* (Oxford, 1985), 669-714.

— and Simms, A. 'Medieval Dublin, 1170-1542' in Moody, T.W., Martin, F.X., and Byrne, F.J., (eds.) *A New History of Ireland*, ix. (Oxford, 1984), 104-6.

—, '*Urbs et suburbium*: beyond the walls of medieval Dublin', in Manning, C. (ed.), *Dublin and Beyond the Pale: Studies in Honour of Patrick Healy* (Bray, 1998), 45-58.

Clarke, M.V., 'William of Windsor in Ireland 1369-76', *Fourteenth Century Studies* (Oxford, 1937).

Cohen, M.N., *Health and the Rise of Civilization* (New Haven, 1988).

Cohn, S.K., 'The place of the dead in Flanders and Tuscany: towards a comparative history of the Black Death' in Gordon, B. and Marshall, P. (eds.), *The Place of the Dead: Death and Remembrance in Late Medieval and Early Modern Europe* (Cambridge, 2000), 17-43.

—, *The Black Death Transformed: Disease and Culture in Early Renaissance Europe* (London, 2002)

Colledge, E. (ed.), *The Latin Poems of Richard Ledrede, OFM, Bishop of Ossory, 1317-1360* (Toronto, 1974).

Conlin, S., *Dublin: One Thousand Years of Wood Quay* (Belfast, 1984)

—, *Historic Dublin* (Dublin 1986).

Connolly, P., 'List of Irish material in the class of Chancery Files, Public Record Office London', Anal. Hib. 31 (1984), 1-18.

—, 'List of Irish material in the class of Ancient Petitions', *Irish Jurist* 18 (1983), 3-106.

—, 'Pleas held before the Chief Governors of Ireland 1308-76', *Irish Jurist* 18 (1983), 101-31.

Coope, G.R., 'Report on the coleoptera from an eleventh-century house at Christ Church Place, Dublin' in H. Bekker-Nielsen, *et al.* (eds), *Proceedings from the Eighth Viking Congress, Aarhus 24-31 August 1977* (Odense, 1981), 51-6.

Corish, P.J., 'The rising of 1641 and the Catholic confederacy, 1641-5' in NHI, iii. 289-316.

—, 'The Cromwellian Conquest, 1649-53' in NHI, iii. 336-352.

Cosgrove, A., *Late Medieval Ireland, 1370-1534* (Dublin, 1981).

–(ed.), *A New History of Ireland, ii: Medieval Ireland 1169-1534* (Oxford, 1987).

—, 'England and Ireland, 1399-1447' in NHI, ii. 525-532.

—, 'The emergence of the Pale, 1399-1447' in NHI, ii. 533-56.

—, 'Ireland beyond the Pale', 1399-1460' in NHI, ii.569-590.

—, 'Parliaments in Ireland, 1264-1800' in Moody, Martin, Byrne (eds.), *A New History of Ireland*, ix (Oxford, 1984), 593-608.

—, 'Chief Governors of Ireland, 1172-1534' in Moody, Martin, Byrne (eds.), *A New History of Ireland*, ix (Oxford, 1984), 469-85.

—, (ed.), *Dublin Through the Ages* (Dublin 1988).

Coughlan, T., 'The Anglo-Norman houses of Dublin: evidence from Back Lane' in Duffy, S. (ed.), *Medieval Dublin I* (Dublin, 2000), 203-34.

Craddock, S., *City of Plagues: Disease, Poverty and Deviance in San Francisco* (Minneapolis, 2000).

Crawford, E.M. (ed.), *Famine: The Irish Experience, 900-1900* (Edinburgh, 1989).

—, 'Typhus in nineteenth-century Ireland' in *Medicine, Disease and the State in Ireland, 1650-1940*, Jones, G. and Malcolm, E. (eds.), (Cork 1999), 121-137.

Crawfurd, R., *Plague and Pestilence in Literature and Art* (Oxford, 1914).

Creighton, C., *A History of Epidemics in Britain* (2 vols., 1891-4, 2nd ed., London 1965).

Cullen, L., 'Economic Trends 1660-1691' in NHI, iii. 387-407.

—, 'The growth of Dublin 1600-1900: character and heritage' in *Dublin City and County: From Prehistory to Present*, Aalen and Whelan (eds.), (Dublin 1992), 251-78.

Cullum, P.H., 'Poverty and charity in early fourteenth-century England' in *England in the Fourteenth Century: Proceedings of the 1991 Harlaxton Symposium*, Rogers, N. (ed.) (Stamford, 1993),140-51.

D'Alton, J., *The History of the County Dublin* (Dublin 1838, reissued 1976).

Dekker, Thomas, 'A Rod for Run-awayes', in Wilson (ed.), *The Plague Pamphlets of Thomas Dekker* (Oxford, 1925), 135-71.

De Vries, J., *European Urbanisation: 1500-1800* (Cambridge, Mass., 1984).

Dickson, D., 'Capital and country: 1600-1800' in Cosgrove (ed.), *Dublin Through the Ages*, 63-76

Dinneen, P.S. (ed.), *Foclóir Gaedhilge agus Béarla: An Irish-English Dictionary* (Dublin, 1927).

Dixon, F.E., 'Weather in old Dublin', Part i, *Dublin Historical Record*, xiii. Nos 3 and 4 (1953), 94-107.

—, 'Weather in old Dublin', Part ii, *Dublin Historical Record*, xv. No 3 (Sept. 1959), 65-73.

Dobson, M., 'Epidemics and the geography of disease' in Loudon, I. (ed.), *Western Medicine: An Illustrated History* (Oxford, 1997), 176-91.

Dohar, W. J., *The Black Death and Pastoral Leadership: The Diocese of Hereford in the Fourteenth Century* (Philadelphia, 1995).

Dols, M.W., *The Black Death in the Middle East* (Princeton, 1977).

Doolin, W., *Dublin's Medical Schools: A Biographical Retrospect* (London, n.d.)

Down, K., 'Colonial society and economy in the high Middle Ages' in NHI, ii. 439-90.

Drancourt, M., *et al.*, 'Detection of 400-year-old *Yersinia pestis* DNA in human dental pulp: an approach to the diagnosis of ancient septicemia', *Proceedings National Academy of Science, USA*, 95 (1998), 12637-40.

Duby, G., *Rural Economy and Country Life in the Medieval West*, trans. Postan. C. (London, 1968).

—, *The Age of Cathedrals* (Chicago, 1980).

Duffy, E., *The Stripping of the Altars: Traditional Religion in England, c. 1400-c. 1580* (New Haven, 1992).

Duffy, S. (ed.), *Medieval Dublin I: Proceedings of the Friends of Medieval Dublin Symposium 2000* (Dublin, 2000).

—, (ed.), *Medieval Dublin II* (Dublin, 2001).

Dunlevy, M., 'The medical families of medieval Ireland' in Doolin, W. and Fitzgerald, O. (eds.) *What's Past is Prologue* (Dublin, 1952), 15-22.

Dyer, C.C., *Standards of Living in the Later Middle Ages* (Cambridge, 1989).

Fleetwood, J.F., *The History of Medicine in Ireland* (Dublin, 1983).

Frame, R., *Colonial Ireland 1169-1369* (Dublin, 1981).

—, *English Lordship in Ireland 1318-1361* (Oxford, 1982).

—, '"Two Kings in Leinster": The Crown and the MicMhurchadha in the fourteenth century' in Barry, Frame and Simms (eds.), *Colony and Frontier in Medieval Ireland* (London, 1995), 155-76.

French, R., *et al.* (eds.), 'Introduction: The "long fifteenth century" of medical history' in French, *Medicine from the Black Death to the French Disease* (Aldershot, 1998), 1-5.

Garcia-Ballester, L., *et al.* (eds.), *Practical Medicine from Salerno to the Black Death* (Cambridge, 1994).

Gasquet, F.A., *The Great Pestilence* (London, 1893).

Geary, P.J., *Living with the Dead in the Middle Ages* (Ithaca, 1994).

Getz, F., *Medicine in the English Middle Ages* (Princeton, 1998).

Gilbert, J.T., *A History of the City of Dublin*, 3 Vols. (Dublin 1854-9, reprinted Dublin, 1978).

—, *Viceroys of Ireland* (Dublin, 1965).

Gilchrist, R., 'Christian bodies and souls: the archaeology of life and death in later medieval hospitals' in *Death in Towns*, Bassett, S. (ed.), (London & New York, 1992), 101-18.

Glasscock, R.E., 'Land and people, c.1300' in NHI, ii. 205-239.

Gordon, B. and Marshall, P. (eds.), *The Place of the Dead: Death and Remembrance in Late Medieval and Early Modern Europe* (Cambridge, 2000).

Gottfried, R.S., *Epidemic Disease in Fifteenth-Century England. The Medical Response and the Demographic Consequences* (New Brunswick, 1978).

—, *The Black Death: Natural and Human Disaster in Medieval Europe* (NY & London, 1983).

—. 'The Black Death' in Strayer *et al.* (eds.), *Dictionary of the Middle Ages* (New York, 1983), ii. 257-67.

Graham, B.J., 'The evolution of urbanisation in medieval Ireland', in *Journal of Historical Geography*, 5 (1979), 111-25.

—, 'Urbanisation in medieval Ireland c.900 to c.1300', *Journal of Urban History*, 13 (1987), 169-96.

—, 'The definition and classification of medieval Irish towns' in *Irish Geography*, 21 (1988), 20-32.

—, 'The high Middle Ages: c.1100 to c.1350' in Graham and Proudfoot (eds.), *An Historical Geography of Ireland* (London, 1993), 58-98.

—, 'Economy and town in Anglo-Norman Ireland' in Bradley (ed.), *Settlement and Society in Medieval Ireland: Studies Presented to F.X Martin* (Kilkenny, 1988), 241-60.

—, 'The towns of medieval Ireland' in Butlin, R.A., (ed.), *The Development of the Irish Town* (London, 1977), 28-59.

–, 'Anglo-Norman colonisation and the size and spread of the colonial town in medieval Ireland', in Clarke, H.B., and Simms, A. (ed.s), *The Comparative History of Urban Origins in Non-Roman Europe* (Oxford, 1985), 355-72.

—, and Proudfoot, L.J. (eds.), *An Historical Geography of Ireland* (London, 1993).

Gransden, A., *Historical Writing in England, ii. c.1307 – early sixteenth century* (London, 1982).

Green, A.S., *The Making of Ireland and its Undoing, 1200-1600* (London, 1908).

Gwynn, A., 'The Black Death in Ireland' *Studies* 24 (1935),25-42.

—, 'Richard FitzRalph, Archbishop of Armagh', *Studies*, 22 (1933), 389-405, 591-607; 23 (1934), 395-411.

—, 'Archbishop FitzRalph and George of Hungary', *Studies*, 24 (1935), 558-72.

–, 'The medieval university of St Patrick's Dublin', *Studies*, 27 (1938), 199-212, 437-54.

—, 'Anglo-Irish church life: fourteenth and fifteenth centuries' in Corish, (ed.) *History of Irish Catholicism*, ii. part iv. (Dublin and Sydney, 1968).

—and Hadcock, R., *Medieval Religious Houses: Ireland* (London, 1970).

Haas, V.H., 'When bubonic plague came to Chinatown', in *American Journal of Tropical Medicine,* 8, 141-47.

Harbison, P., *National Monuments of Ireland* (Dublin, 1970).

Harkness, D. and O'Dowd, M. (eds.), *The Town in Ireland* (Belfast, 1981).

Harper-Bill, C., 'The English church and English religion after the Black Death' in Ormrod and Lindley (eds.), *The Black Death in England* (Stamford, 1996).

Harris, W., *History and Antiquities of the City of Dublin from the Earliest Times* (Dublin, 1765) at http://indigo.ie/~kfinlay/Harris

Hatcher, J., *Plague, Population and the English Economy 1348-1530* (London, 1977) reprinted in *British Population History: from the Black Death to the Present Day*, Anderson, M. (ed.) (New York & Cambridge, 1996), 9-93.

—, 'Mortality in the fifteenth century: some new evidence', in *Economic History Review*, 2nd Series, (1986), 39, 19-38.

—, 'England in the aftermath of the Black Death', in *Past & Present*, 144 (August, 1994), 3-35.

Healy, P., 'The town walls of Dublin', in Clarke (ed.), *Medieval Dublin: The Making of a Metropolis* (Dublin, 1990), 183-92.

Hecker, J., *The Black Death: Epidemics of the Middle Ages*, Babington, B. (trans. and ed.), (1859, reprinted Lawrence, 1972).

Henderson, J., 'The Black Death in Florence: medical and communal responses' in Bassett, S. (ed.), *Death in Towns: Urban Responses to the Dying and the Dead, 100-1600* (London and New York, 1992), 136-50.

Hennessy, M., 'The priory and hospital of New Gate: The evolution and decline of a medieval monastic estate', in Smyth, W.J. and Whelan, K. (eds.), *Common Ground: Essays on the Historical Geography of Ireland* (Cork, 1988), 41-54.

Herlihy, D., *The Black Death and the Transformation of the West*, Cohn, S.K., (ed.), (Cambridge, Mass., 1997).

—, and Klapisch-Zumer, C., *Tuscans and their Families: A Study of the Florentine Catasto of 1427* (New Haven, 1985).

Heuser, W. (ed.), *Die Kildare-Gedichte* (Darmstadt, 1965).

Hibbert, A.B., 'The economic policies of towns', *Cambridge Economic History of Europe*, iii. Postan, *et al.* (eds.) (Cambridge, 1971), 157-229

Hill, J., 'Mayors and Lord Mayors of Dublin, 1229-1447' in Moody, Martin, Byrne (eds.), *A New History of Ireland*, ix (Oxford, 1984), 548-51.

Hirst, L.F., *The Conquest of Plague: A Study of the Evolution of Epidemiology* (Oxford, 1953).

Hoagland, K. (ed.), *1000 Years of Irish Poetry: The Gaelic and Anglo-Irish Poets from Pagan Times to the Present* (NY, 1947).

Hollingsworth, T.H., *Historical Demography* (London, 1969).

— and Hollingsworth, M.F., 'Plague mortality rates by age and sex in the parish of St Botolph's without Bishopsgate, London 1603', *Population Studies*, 25 (1971).

Horrox, R. (ed. and trans.), *The Black Death* (Manchester, 1994).

Hourihane, C., '"Holye Crossys": A catalogue of processional, altar, pendant and crucifix figures for late medieval Ireland', PRIA, 100C (2000), 1-85.

Houston, R.A., *The Population History of Britain and Ireland 1500-1750* (1992), reprinted in Anderson (ed.), *British Population History from the Black Death to the Present Day* (Cambridge, 1996), 99-190.

Huizinga, J., *The Waning of the Middle Ages* (London: Peregrine Books, 1965).

Hunt, J., *Irish Medieval Figure Sculpture, 1200-1600: A Study of Irish Tombs with Notes on Costume and Armour* (Dublin & London, 1974).

Inglesby, T.V., *et al.*, 'Plague as a biological weapon', *Journal American Medical Association*, Vol. 283, No. 17 (3 May 2000), 2281-90.

Jordan, W.C., *The Great Famine: Northern Europe in the Early Fourteenth Century* (Princeton, 1996).

Joyce, J., *Ulysses* (Vintage, New York, 1961).

Joyce, P.W., *The Origin and History of Irish Names of Places* (reprinted Dublin 1995).

Jusserand, J.J., *English Wayfaring Life in the Middle Ages*, Smith, L.T., (trans.), (London, 1889, 4th edition 1950).

Karlen, A., *Plague's Progress: A Social History of Man and Disease* (London, 1995).

Keeling, M. and Gilligan, C., 'Metapopulation dynamics of bubonic plague', *Nature*, 407 (2000), 903-6.

Kelly, J., 'The emergence of scientific and institutional medical practice in Ireland, 1650-1800' in *Medicine, Disease and the State in Ireland, 1650-1940*, Jones, G. and Malcolm, E., (eds.), (Cork 1999), 21-39.

Kelly, M., *A History of the Black Death in Ireland* (Stroud, 2001).

Keen, M., *English Society in the Late Middle Ages 1348-1500* (Harmondsworth, 1990).

Ladurie, E. Leroy, *Times of Feast, Times of Famine: A History of Climate since the Year 1000*, Bray, B. (trans.), (London, 1972).

Langland, William, *Piers the Ploughman*, Goodridge, J.F. (trans.), (Penguin: Harmondsworth, 1970)

Lamb, H.H., *Climate, History and the Modern World* (London, 1982).

Lawlor, H.J., 'Monuments of the pre-Reformation archbishops of Dublin' in Clarke, (ed.), *Medieval Dublin: the Making of a Metropolis* (Dublin, 1990), 227-251.

Lee, G.A., *Leper Hospitals in Medieval Ireland* (Dublin, 1996).

Lennon, C., '"The beauty and the eye of Ireland", the sixteenth century' in Cosgrove, A. (ed.), *Dublin Through the Ages* (Dublin, 1988), 46-62.

Levett, A.E., *Studies in Manorial History* (Oxford, 1938, 2nd ed. 1962).

Little, L.K., *Religious Poverty and the Profit Economy in Medieval Europe* (London, 1978).

Livi-Bacci, M., *A Concise History of World Population*, C. Ipsen, (trans.) (2nd ed. Oxford, 1997).

— , *Population and Nutrition: An Essay on European Demographic History*, T. Croft-Murray and C. Ipsen (trans.) (Cambridge, 1991).

— , *The Population of Europe: A History*. De Nardi Ipsen, C. and Ipsen C. (trans.) (Oxford, 2000).

Logan, 'Pestilence in the Irish wars: the earlier phase', *The Irish Sword*, 7 (1963-4), 279-90.

Loudon, I. (ed.), *An Illustrated History of Western Medicine* (Oxford, 1997).

Lunn, P., 'Nutrition, immunity and infection' in Schofield, R. *et al* (eds.), *The Decline of Mortality in Europe* (Oxford, 1991), 131-45.

Lydon, J., *The Lordship of Ireland in the Middle Ages* (Dublin, 1972).

— , (ed.), *The English in Medieval Ireland* (Dublin, 1972).

— , *Ireland in the Later Middle Ages* (Dublin, 1972).

— , 'A land of war' in NHI , ii. 240-74.

—'The impact of the Bruce invasion, 1315-27', in NHI , ii. 275-302.

—, 'The medieval city' in Cosgrove, A. (ed.), *Dublin Through the Ages*, (Dublin, 1988), 25-45.

—, 'Medieval Wicklow: "A land of war"' in Hannigan, K. and Nolan. W., *Wicklow: History and Society* (Dublin, 1994).

Lyons, M., 'Manorial Administration and the Manorial Economy in Ireland, c.1200-c.1377' (unpublished Ph.D dissertation, Trinity College, Dublin, 1984).

—, 'Weather, famine, pestilence and plague in Ireland, 900-1500' in Crawford, M., *Famine: The Irish Experience* (Edinburgh, 1984), 31-74.

MacArthur, W.P., 'The identification of some pestilences recorded in the Irish annals', in IHS 6 No. 23 (1948-9).

MacGiolla Phádraig, B., 'Fourteenth-century life in a Dublin monastery' in Clarke, H.B. (ed.), *Medieval Dublin: The Living City* (Dublin, 1990), 112-22.

—, 'Speed's Plan of Dublin', part ii, *Dublin Historical Record*, X, No. 4 (June-August 1949), 97-105.

MacLeod, C., 'Some late medieval wood sculptures in Ireland', JRSAI, 77 (1947), 53-62.

Mac Niocaill, G., *Na Buirgeisi*, XII-XV Aois, 2 vols. (Dublin, 1964).

—, 'Socio-economic problems of the late medieval Irish town' in *The Town in Ireland*, Harkness, D. and O'Dowd, M. (eds.) (Belfast, 1981), 5-15.

—, 'The colonial town in Irish documents' in Clarke, H.B., and Simms, A., (ed.), *The Comparative History of Urban Origins in Non-Roman Europe* (Oxford, 1985), 373-8.

Malcolm, E. and Jones, G. (ed.), *Medicine, Disease and the State in Ireland 1650-1940* (Cork, 1999).

Manchester, K., 'The palaeopathology of urban infections' in Bassett (ed.), *Death in Towns* (London & New York, 1995), 8-14.

—, and Roberts, C., *The Archaeology of Disease* (Stroud, 1997).

Manning, C. (ed.), *Dublin and Beyond the Pale: Studies in Honour of Patrick Healy* (Bray, 1998).

McGrath, F.S.J., *Education in Ancient and Medieval Ireland* (Dublin, 1979).

McNeill, C. 'The hospital of St John without the Newgate, Dublin' in JRSAI, 55 (1925), 58-64; reprinted in Clarke, H.B. (ed.) *Medieval Dublin: The Living City* (Dublin 1990), 77-82.

Mc Neill, T.E., 'Church building in fourteenth-century Ireland and the 'Gaelic Revival" in *The Journal of Irish Archaeology*, iii. (1985/6).

McNeill, W. H., *Plagues and Peoples* (Oxford, 1977)

McVaugh, M.R., 'Medicine in the Latin Middle Ages' in Loudon, I. (ed.), *Western Medicine: An Illustrated History* (Oxford, 1997), 54-65.

Meinsma, K.O., *De Zwarte Dood* (Zutphen, 1924).

Meiss, M., *Painting in Florence and Siena after the Black Death* (New York, 1964).

Meyer, K., 'Pneumonic plague', *Bacteriologic Review*, 25 (1961), 249-261.

Miller, E., 'The economic policies of governments' in *The Cambridge Economic History of Europe*, iii., Postan, (ed.) *et al.* (Cambridge, 1971), 281ff.

Millett, B., 'Irish literature in Latin, 1550-1700' in NHI, iii. 561-586.

Mills, J., 'Notices on the manor of St Sepulchure Dublin in the fourteenth century' in JRSAI, 9 (1889), 37-41.

—, 'Tenants and agriculture near Dublin in the fourteenth century' JRSAI, 21 (1891), 54-163.

Mitchell, G., *Archaeology and Environment in early Dublin* (Dublin, 1987).

Mitchell, F., *The Irish Landscape* (London, 1977).

Mollat, M., *Les pauvres au Moyen Âge* (Brussels 1984).

Moody, G.M., and Byrne, (eds.), *A New History of Ireland*, iii (Oxford, 1976); ix (Oxford, 1984).

Moorman, J.R., *A History of the Franciscan Order: From Its Origins to the Year 1517* (Oxford, 1968).

Morris, C., 'The plague in Britain', *The Historical Journal* 14, No. 1 (1971), 205-24.

Moylan, T.K., 'Vagabonds and sturdy beggars: poverty, pigs and pestilence in medieval Dublin' in Clark, H. (ed.), *Medieval Dublin: The Living City* (Dublin, 1990), 192-199.

—, 'Dubliners, 1200-1500', *Dublin Historical Review*, 13 (1952-3), 79-95.

Nic Dhonnchadha, A., 'Medical Writing in Irish', *Irish Journal of Medical Science*, Vol.169, No. 3 (July-Sept. 2000), 217-20.

Nicholas, D., *The Growth of the Medieval City from Late Antiquity to the Early Fourteenth Century* (London & New York, 1997).

—, *Medieval Flanders* (London & New York, 1992).

Nohl, J., *The Black Death: A Chronicle of the Plague compiled from Contemporary Sources*, Clarke, C.H. (trans.) (New York & London, 1924).

Nolan, W. (ed.), *The Shaping of Ireland: The Geographical Perspective* (Cork and Dublin, 1986).

Nutton, V., 'The seeds of disease: an explanation of contagion and infection from the Greeks to the Renaissance,' *Medical History*, 27 (1983), 1-34.

Ormrod, M. and Lindley, P. (eds.), *The Black Death in England* (Stamford, 1996).

Otway-Ruthven, A.J., *A History of Medieval Ireland* (London, 2nd ed. 1980).

— 'The medieval church lands of County Dublin' in *Medieval Studies Presented to A. Gwynn*, Watt, J. *et al.* (eds.) (Dublin, 1961), 54-72.

—, 'The character of the Anglo-Norman settlement in Ireland', in *Historical Studies*, 5 (1965), 75-84.

O' Donnell, E.E., *The Annals of Dublin, Fair City* (Dublin 1987).

O'Meara, T., 'The kingdom of Dalkey' in Anon., *Ireland Sixty Years Ago*, Chapter XI at http://indigo.ie/~kfinlay

Ó Ríordáin, B., 'Excavations at High Street and Winetavern Street, Dublin', in *Medieval Archaeology* 15 (1971), 73-85.

—, 'The High Street excavations' in Clarke (ed.), *Medieval Dublin: The Making of a Metropolis* (Dublin, 1990), 165-72.

O'Sullivan, B., 'The Dominicans in medieval Dublin' in Clarke, H.B. (ed.), *Medieval Dublin: The Living City* (Dublin, 1990), 83-99.

Owst, G.R., *Literature and Pulpit in Medieval England* (Oxford, 2nd ed., 1961).

Park, K., 'Medicine and the Renaissance' in Loudon, I. (ed.), *Western Medicine: An Illustrated History* (Oxford, 1997), 66-79.

Parkhill, J., *et al.*, 'Genome sequence of *Yersinia pestis*, the causative agent of plague,' *Nature*, 413 (4 October 2001), 523-527.

Paterson, R., '*Yersinia* seeks pardon for the Black Death', *Lancet Infectious Diseases*, Vol.2. 6 (2002), 323.

Perrenoud, 'The attenuation of mortality crises and the decline of mortality,' in *The Decline of Mortality in Europe*, Schofield, R., *et al.* (eds.) (Oxford, 1991).

Platt, C., *King Death: The Black Death and Its Aftermath in Late-Medieval England* (London, 1996).

Pollitzer, R. *Plague* (Geneva, 1954).

Porter, Roy, *The Greatest Benefit to Mankind: A Medical History of Humanity from Antiquity to the Present* (London, 1997).

Postan, M., 'Some economic evidence of declining population in the later Middle Ages', *Economic History Review*, 2nd ser. 2 (1950), 130-67.

Poston, R. N., 'Nutrition and Immunity' in Jarret, R.J. (ed.), *Nutrition and Disease* (Baltimore, 1979).

Pounds, N.J.G., *An Historical Geography of Europe, 450BC-AD1330* (Cambridge, 1973).

— , *An Economic History of Medieval Europe* (London, 1974).

Power, C., 'A medieval demographic sample' in Hurley, M.F. and Sheehan, C.M. (eds.), *Excavations at the Dominican Priory, St Mary's of the Isle, Crosse's Green, Cork*, (Cork, 1995), 66-83

Proudfoot and Graham, (ed.), *A Historical Geography of Ireland* (1993).

Prunty, J., 'Improving the urban environment: public health and housing in nineteenth-century Dublin' in Brady and Simms (ed.), *Dublin through Space and Time* (Dublin, 2000).

Rae, E.C., 'Architecture and sculpture, 1169-1603' in NHI, ii. 737-77.

Ranger, T.O. and Slack, P., *Epidemics and Ideas: Essays on the Historical Perception of Pestilence* (Cambridge, 1992).

Raoult, D., *et al.*, 'Suicide PCR/*Yersinia pestis* as cause of the Black Death', in *Proceedings National Academy of Science, USA*, 97.23 (7 November 2000), 12800-12803.

Rawcliffe C., *Medicine and Society in Later Medieval England* (Stroud, 1995).

Razi, Z., *Life, Marriage and Death in a Medieval Parish: Economy, Society and Demography in Halesowen, 1270-1400* (Cambridge, 1980).

Richardson, H.G., and Sayles, G.O., 'Irish revenue 1278-1384', PRIA, 62C (1962), 87-100.

—, (eds.), *Parliaments and Councils of Medieval Ireland* (Dublin, 1947).

—, *The Irish Parliament in the Middle Ages* (Philadelphia, 1952, repr. 1964).

—, *The Administration of Ireland 1172-1377* (Dublin, 1963).

—, Robins, J., *The Miasma: Epidemic and Panic in Nineteenth-Century Ireland* (Dublin, 1995).

Rorig, F., *The Medieval Town* (London, 1967).

Rotberg, R.I. and Rabb, T.K., *Hunger and History* (Cambridge, Mass., 1985).

Russell, J.C., *British Medieval Population* (Albuquerque, 1948)

—, 'Late ancient and medieval populations' in *Transactions of the American Philosophical Society*, 48, part 3 (Philadelphia,1958).

—, 'Late thirteenth-century Ireland as a region', *Demography*, 3, ii. (1966), 500-512.

—, 'Population in Europe, 500-1500', Cipolla, C. (ed.), in *Fontana Economic History of Europe: The Middle Ages* (London, 1972), 25-70.

Salusbury-Jones, G.T., *Street Life in Medieval England* (London, 1975; first pub. 1939).

Sayles, G.O. (ed.), *Documents on the Affairs of Ireland before the King's Council* (Dublin, 1979).

—, 'The legal proceedings against the First Earl of Desmond', Anal. Hib. 23 (1966), 3-47.

Schofield, R., Reher, D. and Bideau, A. (eds.), *The Decline of Mortality in Europe* (Oxford, 1991).

Seymour, St-J., D., *Anglo-Irish Literature, 1200-1582* (Cambridge, 1929).

Shaw, F., 'Medicine in Ireland in medieval times' in Doolin, W. and Fitzgerald O. (eds.), *What's Past is Prologue: A Retrospect of Irish Medicine* (Dublin, 1952), 10-14.

—, 'Medieval medico-philosophical treatises in the Irish language' in Ó Riain (ed.), *Féil-sgríbhinn Eóin Mhic Néill* (Dublin, 1940), 144-57.

Scott, S. and Duncan, C.J., *Biology of Plagues: Evidence from Historical Populations* (Cambridge, 2001).

Shrewsbury, J.F.D., *A History of Bubonic Plague in the British Isles* (Cambridge, 1970).

Simms, A., 'Medieval Dublin: a topographical analysis', *Irish Geography,* 12 (1979), 25-41.

—, 'Medieval Dublin in a European context: from proto-town to chartered town' in Clarke (ed.), *Medieval Dublin: The Making of a Metropolis* (Dublin, 1990), 37-51.

—, 'Continuity and change: settlement and society in medieval Ireland c.500-1500', in Nolan, W. (ed.), *The Shaping of Ireland: The Geographical Perspective* (Cork and Dublin, 1986), 44-65.

—, 'Dublin: Origins and early growth' in Simms and Brady (eds.), *Dublin Through Space and Time* (Dublin, 2000), 15-65.

—, and Brady, J.(eds.), *Dublin Through Space and Time* (Dublin, 2001).

— and Fagan, P., 'Villages in Co. Dublin: their origin and inheritance', in Aalen, F.H.A. and Whelan, K. (eds.), *Dublin City and County: From Prehistory to Present*, 79-119.

—, 'Medieval Dublin 1170-1542' in NHI., ix.

Simms, J.G., 'The Restoration, 1660-85' in NHI. iii. 420-453.

Simpson, L., 'Forty years a-digging: a preliminary synthesis of archaeological investigations in medieval Dublin' in Duffy, S. (ed.), *Medieval Dublin I* (Dublin, 2000), 11-68.

Simpson, W.J., *A Treatise on Plague* (Cambridge, 1905).

Siraisi, N.G., *Medieval and Early Renaissance Medicine: An Introduction to Knowledge and Practice* (Chicago, 1990).

Slack, P., *The Impact of Plague in Tudor and Stuart England* (Oxford, 1990).

de Smet, J.J.(ed.), *Recueil des Chroniques de Flandre*, II (Brussels, 1856).

Smith, R. M., 'Demographic developments in rural England, 1300-1348: a survey', in Campbell, B. (ed.), *Before the Black Death: Studies in the Crisis of the Early Fourteenth Century* (Manchester & New York, 1991), 25-77.

Smyth, W.J. and Whelan, K. (eds.), *Common Ground: Essays on the Historical Geography of Ireland,* (Cork, 1988).

Somerville-Large, P., *Dublin* (London, 1979).

Speed, P. (ed.), *Those Who Worked: An Anthology of Medieval Sources* (New York, 1997).

Stalley, R. A., *Architecture and Sculpture in Ireland, 1150-1350* (Dublin, 1971).

—, 'Gothic art and architecture' in *The Illustrated Archaeology of Ireland* (Dublin, 1991), 172-76.

—, 'Irish Gothic and English fashion', in Lydon (ed.), *The English in Medieval Ireland* (Dublin, 1984), 65-86.

Thompson, J., 'The aftermath of the Black Death and the aftermath of the Great War', *American Journal of Sociology*, 26 (1920-1), 565-72.

Trevalyan, G.H., *English Social History* (London, 1942).

Twigg, G., *The Black Death: a Biological Reappraisal,* (London 1984).

—, '"Plague in London" spatial and temporal aspects of mortality', in *Epidemic Disease in London*, J.A.I. Champion, (ed.) (Centre for Metropolitan History Working Papers Series, No. 1, 1993), 1-17, at

http://www.ihrinfo.ac.uk/cmh/cmh.main.html

Van Bath, S., *Agrarian History of Western Europe, AD 500-1850*, O. Ordish (trans.) (London, 1965).

Van Werveke, H., 'The rise of the towns', *The Cambridge Economic History of Europe*, iii., Postan, *et al.* (eds.) (Cambridge, 1971), 3-41.

—, 'De Zwarte Dood in de Zuidelijke Nederlanden 1349-1351', *Mededelingen van de Koninklijke Vlaamse Akademie voor Wetenschappen: Klasse der Letteren*, 12, 3 (1950).

Verlinden, C., 'Markets and Fairs' in *Cambridge Economic History of Europe*, Vol. III, 119-56.

Wallace, P.F., 'Anglo-Norman Dublin: continuity and change', in O'Corráin, D. (ed.), *Irish Antiquity* (Cork, 1981), 247-67.

—, 'Recent discoveries at Wood Quay', Bull. GSIHS, 5 (1978), 23-6.

—, 'The archaeology of Anglo-Norman Dublin', in Clarke and Simms, (eds.) *Comparative History of Urban Origins in Non-Roman Europe* (Oxford, 1985), 379-410.

—, 'Dublin City: Wood Quay', in *Excavations* (1974), 15-16; 1975-6, 31-2

Walsh, C., *Archaeological Excavations at Patrick, Nicholas and Winetavern Streets, Dublin* (Dingle & Dublin, 1997).

Walsh, K., *A Fourteenth-Century Scholar and Primate: Richard FitzRalph Oxford, Avignon and Armagh* (Oxford, 1981).

Walter, J. and Schofield, R., 'Famine, disease and crisis: mortality in early modern society' in Walter and Schofield (eds.), *Disease and the Social Order in Early Modern Society* (Cambridge, 1989), 1-73.

Warburton, J., Whitelaw, J. and Walsh, R., *History of the City of Dublin* (2 vols.), (London, 1818).

Watt, J.A., 'The Anglo-Irish colony under strain, 1327-99', in NHI iii.352-396.

—, *The Church in Medieval Ireland* (Dublin, 1972).

Watts, S., *Epidemics and History: Disease, Power and Imperialism* (New Haven, 1999).

Weikinn, C., *Quellenkunde zur Witterungsgeschichte Europas von der Zeitwende bis zum Jahre 1850*, vol. i (Berlin, 1958).

Wenzel, S. 'Pestilence and Middle English literature: Friar John Grimestone's poems on death' in Williman (ed.), *The Black Death: The Impact of the Fourteenth-Century Plague* (Binghamton, New York, 1982), 131-59.

Whelan, K., 'The Famine and post-Famine adjustment' in Nolan, W. (ed.), *The Shaping of Ireland* (Cork & Dublin, 1986), 131-164.

Wheelis, M., 'Biological Warfare at the 1346 Siege of Caffa', in *Emerging Infectious Diseases*, Vol. 8, No. 9 (September 2002), 971-5.

WHO, *Plague Manual: Epidemiology, Distribution, Surveillance, and Control* at http://www.who.int/emc-documents/plague

Wilson, F.P. (ed.), *The Plague Pamphlets of Thomas Dekker* (Oxford, 1925).

Wood, H., 'The office of Chief Governor of Ireland, 1172-1509', PRIA, 36C. (1921-4), 206-38.

Ziegler, P., *The Black Death* (London, 1969).

Zinsser, H., *Rats, Lice and History* (Boston, 1965).

List of Illustrations

ILLUSTRATIONS WITHIN THE TEXT

PICTURE SECTIONS

Index